A COSTLY OBEDIENCE

A COSTLY OBEDIENCE

Sermons by
Women of
Steadfast Spirit

edited by
Elizabeth Smith Bellinger

Judson Press ® Valley Forge

A Costly Obedience: Sermons by Women of Steadfast Spirit
© 1994
Judson Press, Valley Forge, PA 19482-0851

Bible quotations in this volume are from the NEW REVISED STANDARD VERSION of the Bible, copyrighted 1989 by the Division of Christian Education of the National Council of the Churches of Christ in the United States of America, and are used by permission. All rights reserved. HOLY BIBLE: *New International Version,* copyright © 1973, 1978, 1984. Used by permission of Zondervan Bible Publishers. The Revised Standard Version of the Bible, copyright © 1946, 1952, 1971, by the Division of Christian education of the National Council of the Churches of Christ in the USA. Used by permission. *The New English Bible.* Copyright © The Delegates of the Oxford University Press and The Syndics of the Cambridge University Press 1961, 1970. *The Holy Bible,* King James Version.

Selections reprinted with permission from:
Meditations with Mechtild of Magdeburg, edited by Sue Woodruff, Copyright 1982, Bear & Co., Inc., P.O. Drawer 2860 Santa Fe, NM 87504.

THE PANTHER AND THE LASH by Langston Hughes
Copyright 1951 by Langston Hughes. Reprinted by permission of Alfred A. Knopf, Inc.

Library of Congress Cataloging-in-Publication Data

A costly obedience : sermons by women of steadfast spirit / edited by
    Elizabeth Smith Bellinger.
        p. cm.
Includes bibliographical references.
ISBN 0-8170-1205-2
1. Sermons, American—Women authors. 2. Southern Baptist Convention—Sermons.
    3. Baptists—Sermons. I. Bellinger, Elizabeth Smith, 1948-
BX6333.A1C67 1994
252'.06132-dc20   93-45873

Printed in the U.S.A.

94 95 96 97 98 99 00 01   8 7 6 5 4 3 2 1

Dedication

This book is dedicated to my daughter, Gillian Kathleen, who, in her search for God, preached her first sermon at age nine:

Does God really love us, or does he truly love us? God always showed himself in different ways. He would show himself as a burning bush or a dove. It is as if he cared then and helped us then. Now he never does anything himself, except when he shows himself in your mind.

How do you know that he is not your conscious? When he does not show himself, it feels as if he were not there for you when you need someone to love you. I wonder if he loved the people of old he showed himself to, or did he truly love them? And he only shows people he truly loves. Or is he not real, and the Bible is one big fat lie.

Is God real or not?

Preached April 1989 at
Lake Shore Baptist Church
Waco, Texas

May Gillian experience the Presence, and may what we do have meaning for this generation and generations to come as they search for God.

98718

Contents

Foreword

It is perhaps the most tragic contradiction of Christendom that the "isms" of race, gender, class, and the myriad forms of oppression that bigotry breeds have been allowed to invade and too often thrive in the household of faith. Further, it is indeed a theological and denominational scandal that among Baptists—that group of Christians who historically have held freedom of conscience and courage of religious conviction to be as sacred as believers baptism—women who confess that they have experienced the call of God to preach the Good News of the gospel of Jesus Christ are met with gross institutional opposition.

Therefore, this collection of sermons by Southern Baptist women preachers is indeed an offering of *Costly Obedience*. These preachers, with their many thousand sister preachers across the church could not have imagined how rugged a road they were choosing when they answered yes to that call of Christ. They were faced with two choices: the living death of denial and disobedience or the rough path of rejection and pain. They chose obedience, a costly obedience. These sermons reflect the paradoxes of their choice. They are voices crying in the wilderness that is inside the church, "Prepare ye the way of the Lord. In this desert make God's pathway straight." The pulpit provides for them no safe haven from suffering, but they are able to take the risks and stand the trial because the Christ they preach, the Christ they obey, is indeed the Christ—Savior for the world and for obedient sister preachers.

The great irony of this rough and risky relationship between women preachers and the churches is that without the radical obedience to Christ that characterizes the ministries of these faithful preachers, the "isms" threaten to utterly extinguish the altar fire. God is gifting the church at this peculiar hour in its history with consecrated women who are, in the words of Anne Thomas Neil, charged to be "Keepers of the Fire." The church is therefore challenged to hear them or risk the removal of its lamp stand from the altar (Revelation 2). And as keepers of the fire, women preachers are challenged to withstand the trial of sexism and to use that experience to help the church to remove every "ism," every idolatry which threatens to extinguish the sacred flame.

> *...the uneven ground shall become level, and the rough places a plain. Then the glory of the LORD shall be revealed, and ALL PEOPLE shall see it together, for the mouth of the LORD has spoken."*
> *(Isaiah 40:4b-5, emphasis added)*

Prathia Hall Wynn
United Theological Seminary
Dayton, Ohio

Preface

This collection of sermons articulates the callings, purposes, and visions of Baptist women in ministry through the 1980s and 1990s. These decades were difficult ones for some women in ministry. Until recently, women in Baptist history were for the most part lost to us. We are just now learning some of their names and reiterating their deeds. Occasionally an example of these hidden heroes surfaces to remind us of countless others whose faces we have not seen and whose names we do not know. May the sermons collected here reflect a memory for those countless others who have gone before us as obedient and faithful servants of the Word.

The first six sermons in this volume were preached during the times of worship that were part of the annual meetings of Southern Baptist Women in Ministry. The other sermons are taken from worship settings that reflect the diversity and power of God's Word for differing times and places.

This collection of sermons does not pretend to speak for all women and men, but it does invite a wide readership to listen to the Word God has shared through these few Baptist preachers. In all parts of the church, many women—and more than a few men—seek ways of liberating the Word in order to speak the gospel. It is hoped that *A Costly Obedience* will provide resources for collective discussion in Bible study, teaching, and preaching, as well as personal study and meditation. As we join together in our study of the Bible, may we be surprised by the fresh insights and challenges that arise as we read and listen to these sermons and search out the meaning of the texts for our own lives.

May those who have ears to hear, hear the Word of God expressed in these sermons and be renewed and sustained.

Contributors

NANCY ELLETT ALLISON is serving as Chaplain at Baylor Medical Center, Dallas, Texas. She earned the Master of Divinity degree and the Ph.D. from Southwestern Baptist Seminary, Fort Worth, Texas. She was ordained to the gospel ministry by Royal Lane Baptist Church, Dallas, Texas, in 1981.

VIRGINIA C. BARFIELD is based in Charlotte, North Carolina, while she learns to live with a medical disability and continues to do research for a doctorate at Duke University. She earned her Master of Divinity at Southeastern Baptist Theological Seminary, Wake Forest, North Carolina. She was ordained to the gospel ministry by Oakland Avenue Baptist Church, Rock Hill, South Carolina, in 1981.

ELIZABETH SMITH BELLINGER is serving as assistant director of Central Texas Senior Ministry, Waco, Texas. She earned the Master of Divinity and D.Min. degrees from Southeastern Baptist Seminary, Wake Forest, North Carolina. She was ordained to the gospel ministry by the First Baptist Church, Lexington, North Carolina, in 1975.

JAN FULLER CARRUTHERS is Chaplain of the College at Hollins College, Roanoke, Virginia. She served in a similar capacity at Yale University, New Haven, Connecticut. She earned a Master of Divinity degree at the Divinity School at Yale and was ordained to the gospel ministry by Trinity Baptist Church, New Haven, Connecticut, in 1981.

JANN ALDREDGE-CLANTON is serving as Chaplain at Baylor Baptist Medical Center, Dallas, Texas. She earned her Master of Divinity at Southwestern Baptist Theological Seminary, Fort Worth, Texas, and her M.A. and Ph.D. degrees at Texas Christian University.

She was ordained to the gospel ministry by Seventh and James Baptist Church, Waco, Texas, in 1985.

NANCY HASTINGS SEHESTED is Pastor at Prescott Memorial Baptist Church, Memphis, Tennessee. She earned her Master of Divinity at Union Theological Seminary, New York, and was ordained to the gospel ministry by Oakhurst Baptist Church, Decatur, Georgia, in 1981.

CINDY HARP JOHNSON is Executive Director of Bread for the Journey Proclamation Ministries, located in Gaithersburg, Maryland. She earned her Master of Divinity at Southern Baptist Theological Seminary, Louisville, Kentucky, and was ordained to the gospel ministry by Wolf Creek Baptist Church, Kentucky, in 1984.

SUSAN LOCKWOOD is Pastor at St. Luke's Baptist Church, Gainesville, Georgia. She earned her Master of Divinity degree from the Southern Baptist Theological Seminary, Louisville, Kentucky. She was ordained to the gospel ministry by Deer Park Baptist Church, Louisville, Kentucky, in 1983.

BETTY WINSTEAD MCGARY is serving as Assistant Pastor at Calder Baptist Church, Beumont, Texas. She earned an M.A. in Christian Education from Southern Seminary, Louisville, Kentucky. Her Ed.D. was earned at the University of Louisville. She was ordained to the gospel ministry by Crescent Hill Baptist of Louisville, Kentucky, in 1985.

MOLLY MARSHALL is Associate Professor of Theology at the Southern Baptist Theological Seminary, Louisville, Kentucky. She earned her Master of Divinity and Ph.D. degrees from Southern. She was ordained to the gospel ministry by St. Matthews Baptist Church in Louisville, Kentucky, in 1983.

LEIGH Q. MOSEMAN is serving as Chaplain for Central Texas Senior Ministry, Waco, Texas. She earned the Master of Divinity degree from Southern Baptist Theological Seminary, Louisville, Kentucky. She was ordained to the gospel ministry by the First Baptist Church, Hartselle, Alabama, in 1989.

ANNE THOMAS NEIL is a Missionary Emerita from the Southern Baptist Foreign Mission Board. She has served as Visiting Professor of Missions at Southeastern Seminary, Wake Forest, North Carolina, and as President of the Southern Baptist Alliance. She is a graduate of Mather School of Nursing (R.N.), Southern Baptist Theological Seminary (M.R.E.), and Western Kentucky University (Ed.S.).

SHARLANDE SLEDGE is Associate Pastor of Lake Shore Baptist Church, Waco, Texas. She earned the Master of Religious Education degree from Southwestern Baptist Seminary, Fort Worth, Texas, and was ordained to the gospel ministry by Lake Shore Baptist Church, Waco, Texas, in 1987.

LYNDA WEAVER-WILLIAMS is Adjunct Professor of New Testament at Virginia Commonwealth University, Richmond, Virginia. She earned her Master of Divinity and Ph.D. degrees at Southern Baptist Theological Seminary, Louisville, Kentucky. She was ordained to the gospel ministry by Goshen Baptist Church, Goshen, Kentucky, in 1981.

We Have This Treasure

2 Corinthians 4:7-18

Nancy Hastings Sehested

Greetings to you, sisters and brothers, in the name of our Lord Jesus Christ, who did not count equality with God a thing to be grasped; in the name of our Lord, who no longer calls us servants but friends; in the name of our Lord, who welcomed Mary to his teaching, saying that she had chosen the good portion, the one thing that was needed.

Wherever the Spirit of Christ rules, there is freedom! Wherever the Holy Spirit blows, the neat corners and taut strings on the package created to box God in are torn and unraveled. Our ancestors in the faith lived in tents that could easily be broken down and carried on the journey to a new land and a new home. The tabernacle itself was portable—God would not be enclosed with bricks and mortar, stone and wood.

Our spiritual pilgrimage as women is like the lives of our spiritual ancestors. As the Hebrews passed out of bondage and slavery in Egypt, there was great anticipation, great excitement, a vision of new lives and new possibilities. A new land. A new place.

Ah, but then there was the desert. The expectation and vision of a new place, a new way of living, came crashing into the experience of the desert. Maybe Egypt wasn't so bad after all. At least we could eat.

Sweet Egypt. You remember, don't you, Moses?

Sweet Egypt. What I wouldn't give for a leg of roasted lamb and a pitcher full of wine!

Sweet Egypt. The expectation of freedom fades from memory under the grueling desert road.

Sweet Egypt. What a fool I must have been to think of anything better than slavery! What a mistake to be tricked into thinking that God had anything more in store for me, that my sweat and labor could belong to anyone other than my master's slave taskmaster—that, in fact, it could belong to me and be put toward the service of One whom no pharaoh may rule.

Ah, sweet Egypt. Someone told me Moses tended sheep here in the desert before he took to preaching on street corners in the city. I think the combined effect of the smell and the heat must have scrambled his brain. Land of milk and honey and promise—hah!

Sweet, sweet Egypt. Think old master Pharaoh would take us back?

Think with me for a minute. In what ways have your expectations—your hopes and dreams and callings and visions—been preyed upon and victimized by your experience of attempting to live them out in flesh and blood?

The Scripture passage you've heard read from 2 Corinthians this morning is a good one for us to dwell on. In fact, Paul's famous image—"We have this treasure in earthen vessels"—is worth considering as a mirror to reflect on our common spiritual pilgrimage. I'd like to suggest something of a novel way of entering into the text: starting at midpoint, moving backwards to the beginning and then confronting the end.

Before anything else, there is the treasure. Before anything else, the undifferentiated Good News. Gospel news. News of God's grace. And not just news, as in information, but news as in experience. And not just a word, but the Word, in living color, flesh and blood, a walking portrait of divine mercy and forgiveness and promise. But there's more still. Not just Good News generally, but Good News—treasure—for us, for me. Not just timeless, cosmic, nameless Good News, but Good News for me, with my name on it, in my life. The Good News gets specific. It calls my name and bids me to follow.

And I say, "Who, me? You gotta be kidding. I'm a woman! I've got a high voice and no hair on my chest. I'm emotional, I cry, and I can't think straight. I prefer cooking and diapers and diets and cleaning up after Wednesday night church suppers. At least I'm supposed to, am I not?"

Maybe yes, maybe no. What does it matter? Martha wasn't distracted with serving, but with much serving; she was anxious and troubled about many things, but not the one thing needed. She was blocked by unseen forces, from choosing the "good portion." Old Pharaoh would have liked her. Every busy pastor would love to have a stable of Marthas.

But stables are for horses. Not women. Not men.

But back to Paul and treasure—our treasure—not as a thing to be grasped, but a call to a new order of service, as different from the old as night is from day, as east is from west. We have this treasure.

But there's trouble in paradise. We have this treasure in earthen vessels. We share this "earthen vessel" quality—this not-yet-perfected, this not-yet-mature, this not-yet-fully-refined quality—along with all others whose names have been called, whose hearts have been gripped, whose devotion has been commanded.

And our fellow earthen vessels look at us much the way James and the other leaders of the first church at Jerusalem must have looked at Paul when he first suggested he go over and preach to the Gentiles.

Gentiles in the fellowship? Women in the ministry?

You're gonna baptize a what? You're gonna ordain a what?

The uncircumcised at our table? Skirts in our pulpit?

Putting treasures in earthen vessels is something like putting an ice-cream cone in two-year-old hands. Things can get messy.

How are we to live, how are we to carry on, how are we to keep hope alive when visionary expectation intersects with the concrete details of this time and this place and our lives?

Were we foolish to come here? If not foolish, maybe just misguided? If we spoke loudly enough to be heard doors away and blocks away, we would certainly be met with a chorus of yeses. Old master Pharaoh will take us back if we're good girls and learn to behave ourselves.

But most of us just feel trapped. We feel afflicted, perplexed, persecuted, and struck down—sometimes even on the edge of being crushed, driven to despair, forsaken, and destroyed. We simply can't go back. Our eyes have been opened and our ears have popped. The way back is blocked by a force far greater than Pharaoh's army. But so far the future only chokes us with dust and blinds us with sand. These desert storms give us a bad case of spiritual dyslexia, spiritual disorientation, not knowing which way is forward and which is backward.

With these experiences fresh in our minds—sometimes even branded upon our hearts—we come to Paul's affirmation of hope, his

vital sense of expectation, with a certain measure of puzzlement. And
with a discreet tone of voice, we ask, "Run that by me again?"

"Afflicted . . . , but not crushed; perplexed, but not driven to
despair; persecuted, but not forsaken; struck down, but not destroyed"
(2 Corinthians 4:8-9). We can get into the part about being given up
to death for Jesus' sake. But Paul continues in verse 16: "So we do not
lose heart."

The first thing that comes to mind as a response is: Says who?

Sisters and brothers, Paul is saying, here is my testimony. May God
bless and use these words as is needed and fitting.

We live in the great in-between time. We are ready, but still waiting.
We are called, but not confirmed. We are trained, but not employed.
We are willing, but not able.

Pastors tell us their congregations are not yet ready and able to
accept us. Congregations tell us their pastors are not yet ready and
able to accept us. We are to our convention like Paul's early Gentile
converts.

We live in the great in-between time. Our calling is clear, and our
gifts are manifest. But the desert is a severe, unforgiving place. Many
have already parted company, taking on other careers in other fields
or taking positions with other denominations. Are there many among
us who have not entertained such options? For those who have moved
on, we bid Godspeed. Some of us feel that if we had any sense, we
would do the same. But we remain. It is no special virtue, no special
righteousness. Stiff upper lips won't do. We can't fully understand why
we stay, although all of us would have some partial reasons. The
deepest reason is not fully fathomable. The best we can say is that this
is where we're called to be. And that's enough.

We live in the great in-between time. We hope for brighter futures,
assured of nothing but God's continued fidelity to undergird our
spirits and nurture our souls. We see glimmers of light here and there
shining in the darkness, and we celebrate and cultivate the light. But
we know that light shines from a great distance. It will be a while yet
before the whole room is lit up.

We live in the time of great in-between. I propose that we make a
covenant with each other: That we covenant to care for each other, to
listen to each other, to be open to each other's encouragement and

counsel. That we stay in touch with each other, allow each other the freedom to make different choices, burn our bitterness as a sacrifice to the Lord.

That we confess to each other, treat each other with gentleness.

That we open our communion to new brothers as well as sisters. That we pray for each other, challenge each other, rejoice with each other, weep with each other.

That we covenant to meet again with each other, for mutual support and correction, for study of the Scriptures with each other, for singing spiritual songs and hymns together.

Why? Because we have this treasure. We have this treasure in earthen vessels—vessels that need filling and refilling again and again. Vessels filled to spill over with healing waters to a hurting world.

The treasure is not buried. It is here among us and in us.

For what we preach is not ourselves, but Jesus Christ as Lord.

We are afflicted in every way, but not crushed.

Perplexed, but not driven to despair.

Persecuted, but not forsaken.

Struck down, but not destroyed.

Let the light shine in our hearts.

Let the light shine on out of darkness.

For we have this treasure.

This sermon was preached at the June 1983 meeting of the Southern Baptist Women in Ministry in Pittsburgh, Pennsylvania.

Exercising Our Gifts:
A Question of Obedience

Matthew 10:16-33

Susan Lockwood

We all grow up with certain preconceived ideas about how life, and even faith, should be.

Many of us, if not consciously, at least subconsciously, believe that life should be fair, religious institutions should be just, and faith should be easy. Part of growing into maturity as persons and as Christians, however, is coming to terms with the brutal realities that life is not always fair, that religious institutions are not always just, and that faith is not always easy.

No matter how good we are, cancer can strike us down. No matter how hard we study and how much we achieve, certain opportunities will be denied us. No matter how much we pray, faith does not eliminate opposition.

This is not intended to be a cynical appraisal of life in general or of God and religious life in particular. Certainly the gospel message is one of hope and Good News. But much of the pain that I have experienced personally as a woman minister, and that I see in other women and men in ministry, leads me to conclude that if we are to remain faithful in the exercising of our gifts, then we must take a closer look at what the claims of the gospel mean to the actual living out of our lives.

I make this brash statement as I observe not only women, but also men, leaving our denomination and even the faith because of frustration and alienation. I do not speak in judgment of them but as one who has grappled at length with this same problem. Neither do I offer this as a facile statement from one who "has it made." As I have sat through numerous meetings where brothers and sisters in Christ have denounced my ministry, rejected my call, and accused me of heresy or worse, I have often been discouraged—pushed to doubt and the brink of despair. The calls, letters, and words of support have helped. But in the final analysis, it has come down to whether or not I will follow Jesus Christ.

Having said this, let me hasten to add that if there is any one thing that I have come to grasp more fully in the last nine months, it is that following the Christ of the Gospels is no easy matter. And it is to this fact that our text speaks so poignantly.

In instructing the disciples as to how they are to go out, Jesus issues a dark warning to all his followers: I am sending you out as sheep in the midst of wolves. You will be delivered up to councils, flogged by religious institutions, and even dragged into court—all for the sake of following me. Jesus further forewarns his followers that their faith may create division and strife among family members.

These warnings were tragically fulfilled in the first century. Can the cost of following Jesus Christ now be any less than the cost of following Jesus Christ in the first century?

If we are to be disciples of Jesus Christ, can we expect to escape the trials and sufferings that the original disciples faced? However, the fact that so few Christians and churches risk public scorn may be an indictment of our practice of Christianity. As Dietrich Bonhoeffer wrote in 1938, grace that calls to discipleship is costly because it can cost a person her own life, his own life—in the first century, in 1938, and now. This is precisely why most of us, including myself, have little desire for Christian discipleship: it has consequences, and we are afraid.

Now fear, in and of itself, is not necessarily a bad thing. It serves the function of self-preservation. It is a natural and necessary instinct in many situations. But fear, like other helpful, self-preservative, natural instincts, must be controlled, must be subjected to discipline. Otherwise, it becomes dangerous; it stands in the way of our following our Lord.

The Scripture tells us, though, that we need not be anxious when we are placed in these difficult situations. That doesn't mean that we never feel scared; we're not, after all, called to be stupid. Jesus' words to us are: "Be wise as serpents and innocent as doves" (Matthew 10:16).

One preacher calls it "acting with compassionate shrewdness."[1] This means that we don't court martyrdom, but neither do we allow our fear to stand in the way of living out our divine calling—even if we as women respond to a call that is misunderstood or met with resistance.

Our text offers us several promises as we act in defiance of our fears:[2]

First, we are promised that if we cannot escape persecution, we can trust God to help us through it. We are reassured that God will supply both the words to say and the courage to speak them. We need not be afraid to deliver any speech. We need not worry about the manner or substance of our reply to the charges of our persecutors. God can speak through us, furnishing us with both courage and testimony.

Second, our testimony will mightily proclaim the kingdom of God. You see, Christian witness is not mere verbal assent but a demonstration—the witness of a life lived at great risk. It is this kind of testimony that becomes the channel through which the kingdom is made visible and present in this world.

And third, this kind of trust in God, this faith, will be our salvation—"the one who endures to the end will be saved" (Matthew 10:22). It is by remaining faithful through this process of refinement that salvation comes. This kind of trust also saves us from the hell of cowardice and the hell of guilt. We will not have to live with the inward chaos created by denying the truth. Neither will we have to carry the burden of trusting in ourselves.

But it seems unfair, doesn't it, that a person should have to suffer and be persecuted for following Jesus Christ?

If salvation is a free gift, why is the cost so high? Why is it that pain must accompany salvation, that the alternative to hell must often hurt, that the cure looks as bad to us as the disease?

Verses 24 and 25 of our text point out that Jesus himself was called the devil and was persecuted. We all know the ultimate pain he bore. Why should we his disciples expect less? Is the disciple above the teacher? the servant above the master? We are not to expect better treatment than our Lord. If we follow Jesus Christ, we can expect what he received: friends, joy, a mission—and pain, abandonment, and a nasty, dirty, disgraceful cross.

So we are called to be willing to endure persecution. What does this mean? How are we to act when threatened for the sake of the gospel? Is there a Christian style of suffering? The words "fear not" appear three times in verses 26 through 31. We are encouraged not to be immobilized or turned aside by our fear. We are challenged to act with a confidence that may appear mysterious to those around us. While the message of Jesus Christ may seem to reach only a few, God will see to it that our efforts have great effect.

In addition, Jesus enjoins his disciples to proclaim publicly what he has taught them in small groups. What was told in the dark is now to be uttered in the light; what was once whispered is now to be shouted from the housetops. Discipleship, even in the presence of fear, must be acknowledged, practiced, and proclaimed in public. It is not a private affair, even though the world's response to public proclamation may be hostile.

Of whom, then, are we to be afraid? Jesus said not to fear those who kill the body—for after that, there is nothing else they can do. But we are to fear God, who ultimately controls our destiny.

Eternal consequences, which are sometimes hard for us to see, are far greater than the temporal ones that loom so large before us, said our Lord. And Jesus is not speaking merely about gaining heaven in the "sweet by-and-by." Eternal consequences can begin in the sour here and now.

A German theologian urges us to think about the silence of churches when synagogues went up in flames forty years ago in Germany, when Jews who worshiped in those synagogues were mass-murdered. He observes that the scars we all bear to this day are massive; there is national and world guilt; there is alienation. One who lived through the Holocaust said, "If I deny the truth, if I permit injustice, if I take no notice of the people who are being persecuted—then my family and I will get along the better for it; but the torments of hell begin at the same time—the torments of a broken backbone and unforgivable guilt."[3]

By the same token, church leaders and Christians who fail to speak out and be counted when the calls of women ministers are challenged may get along better by avoiding the controversy, but they will have to live with the realization that their silence may perpetuate injustice. Women who fail to respond to frightening calls may have a smoother road for the moment, but later may have to travel the bumpy road of regret.

So it appears we are caught between the devil and the deep blue sea, between a rock and a hard place. Down one fork in the road lies separation from a God who made us and loves us. But take the other fork, and there's pain, there's loneliness; there are all kinds of threats that we could avoid by going the other way.

So what do we have to help us choose? If we pick the straight and narrow way, the one that we are told leads to light and life, what can we expect?

For one thing, we can expect the care of a God who notices and feels the plight of small birds, of a God who knows how many hairs we have on our heads.

For another, we are promised protection in all circumstances. Often what we want is protection from circumstances, from dangers and toils and snares. Instead, we're offered strength and solace and ultimate victory in those circumstances.

And most important, we are promised that Jesus will be our advocate before God who is in heaven—that our faithfulness in bearing witness to Jesus Christ will be met with Christ's faithfulness in bearing witness of us to God.

It isn't easy to be a woman minister today, as well I know. The pain of rejection and controversy seems to surround our every action. It truly isn't fair that we are subjected to such adversity when all we want to do is to exercise to the fullest the gifts that God has given us. And it isn't fair that we are denied access to certain positions and areas of ministry simply because we were born female.

If we look at the picture of discipleship painted by today's text, we see that full conformity to following Jesus Christ is not a matter of fairness or ease but of a willingness to follow at any cost—even that of our lives.

As God instructed Moses: Let us move forward in faith!

This sermon was preached at the June 1984 meeting of the Southern Baptist Women in Ministry in Kansas City, Missouri.

NOTES

1. George Buttrick, *Interpreter's Bible VII* (Nashville: Abingdon Press, 1951), 367-373.

2. The following three points are taken from Buttrick, *Interpreter's Bible VII:* 367-373.

3. Jürgen Moltmann, *Power of the Powerless* (New York: Harper & Row, 1982), 83.

Singing the Lord's Song

Psalm 137:1-4, Colossians 3:12-17

Molly Marshall

In a way, to preach on "singing the Lord's song" may seem to some to be crying "peace where there is no peace." And yet for others it might presuppose that the journey out of exile is complete for us all. And we know that is not the case.

To be in exile suggests somehow that once we were all in Zion, living in the perfect community indicative of the messianic age. But that is not true, for much of the Christian vision lies out ahead of us, yet to be claimed. The church, especially its women, has not made it to the Promised Land. A "repristinization" of the past should not be our goal. The "good ol' days" weren't good for everybody! "Sighing for Eden" (to borrow the title of William Willimon's fine book) cripples the eschatological march into the future God prepares with and for us. Our yearning gaze and efforts should be toward the horizon God places before us rather than with days gone by. Thus, "How can I forget thee, Jerusalem" is not our theme, but a new song, full of hope and promise.

What are we to be about during these storm-tossed days as Baptists? Most of us here are not without firm opinions about the role of women in ministry. (My father used to say, "Daughter, are you always so sure?") Of this I am very sure: our meeting is prophetic in itself, but we have other concerns as well. We hunger for direction in what it means to be the people of God at this critical juncture in the life of our respective churches and in our convention as a whole. We long for our rhetoric to become enfleshed in constructive, transforming actions. Yet many of us feel powerless and voiceless even in the face of God's beckoning Spirit. Our hearts echo the lament of the psalmist: "How can we sing the Lord's song in a foreign land?" Or to paraphrase a bit, "How can we sing the Lord's song—that is, celebrate Christ's victory in our living—when the true homeland is not yet in sight?"

The writer of Colossians is not without a hopeful word. Indeed, he answers the poignant question of the psalmist. There is a way to live that will make a radical difference in the lives of all around you, no matter what the circumstances, Paul suggests. It is to cultivate the qualities that were preeminently displayed in the life of Jesus—in other words, to "put on Christ." Men and women of the new creation, God's chosen people, set apart for service, into whose hearts he has poured his love, should inevitably reflect something of Christ's nature. "Singing the Lord's song" is manifesting the Christian graces in the face of injustice, unrighteousness, and hopelessness. It is a proactive stance.

The text spells out these graces: compassion, kindness, humility, gentleness, patience, and forgiveness. These words seem to lack the evocative sizzle of words that are shrewd, dominant, urgent, retaliatory, profound—they seem powerless by comparison. Yet, are these not the qualities of Jesus, in whose very being the power of God is most fully revealed? Could it be that as we are compassionate or gentle or forgiving or even patient that we are displaying the same mighty power that raised Christ from the dead? Could it be that the strongest thing that we do is to "sing the Lord's song" in the face of all adversity, believing that "we are more than conquerors through him that loved us?" Of course, to the cynical, such would seem little more than Jiminy Crickett's instruction to "give a little whistle" when afraid. What an absurd posture—like "breaking bread on the abyss," like eating a meal with his disciples even as the cross loomed, like continuing to serve even when motives and theological posture are suspect.

In one of her most insightful books, *The Strength of the Weak*, Dorothee Söelle warns us not to trade apathy for suffering. There is that tendency, isn't there? We get weary pushing on the same old barriers erected by sinful humanity and are tempted to say, "It doesn't matter anyway." "Apathy as the denial of suffering in one's own inner life" becomes "apathy as the incapacity to feel sympathy for others."[1] We become tired of feeling our own pain, and a "headlong flight from suffering" seems attractive. As Kolakowski notes in *Presentness of Myth*, "Apathy, an absence of suffering, and the desire to go through life without experiencing pain are all hallmarks of the culture dominant in the First World."[2] It's just easier to avoid the inevitable conflict that following Jesus incurs.

"Singing the Lord's song" means that we must continue to confront the sources of inequality, bigotry, and dehumanization—feeling our own pain and the pain of others. To have compassion is "the knowledge that there can never really be any peace and joy for me until there is peace and joy finally for you too," in Frederick Buechner's spare and piercing words.[3] We are accountable to one another—yes, we are our "brother's keeper" (in the generic sense!).

Paul wrote during a time that was no less divided than our own. He prefaced the passage we are highlighting by asserting, "Here there is no Greek and Jew, circumcised or uncircumcised (that must refer to the women!), barbarian, Scythian, slave or free; but Christ is all, and is in all" (Colossians 3:11, NIV). Of course all these categories did not all at once magically disappear, but they did learn to see them as something other than insurmountable hindrances to unity in Christ. However, such unanimity required that each "put on Christ," with each acting with the encompassing love, forbearance, and humility of their Lord.

Our world is crossed and recrossed by lines of enmity of one kind or another, and our lives are scarred by the animosities we nurse. In the unity of the life in Christ, there is no room for old cleavages, for unreconciled disparity. This "restoration of the original image of creation"[4] will yet be universally displayed, but how good and pleasant it is when here and now that day of the revelation of the daughters and sons of God is anticipated as we "sing the Lord's song" together. When Christ's peace becomes the arbiter in our hearts, our divided world is confronted with a witness more eloquent than all our preaching and feels constrained to say, as in Tertullian's time, "See how they love one another."[5]

We must learn that when we "put on Christ," we are committing our lives to a different form of change agency that requires our vulnerability. "Jesus is the revelation," according to McGill, "that God's . . . sovereignty does not consist in . . . domination over men [and women], but in his self-giving his own life to them."[6] And such is required of us, even though it is a form of leadership many have not witnessed.

When I was pastor of the Jordan Baptist Church in Sanders, Kentucky, we had a terrible problem in the extended children's session during the worship service. The children liked to "play church" during that time; however, the little girls would not let the little boys be the "preacher." Ida B. would patiently instruct the bossy girls, "Now, little boys can be preachers, too!" But, of course, they hadn't seen one and weren't too sure it was possible!

Many persons who observe the churches of which we are a part have had little opportunity to view relationships clothed in Christ, evidenced in loving, grateful, unselfish ministry. Our witness has more often been tarnished by arguments of who's in charge and actions that betray that our hearts are curved in upon ourselves, as Augustine described human nature.

"Singing the Lord's song" means that our lives are marked by the grace of gratitude, a visible sign to broken humanity of God's loving, redemptive mission. We must live as if our faith has become sight if our world is to have even a glimpse of what it means to live as God intended. Can we celebrate the kingdom's nearness even now? We are doing just that as we gather to affirm our desire to implement the gospel fully.

Grant that we may not be afraid!

This sermon was preached in June 1985 in Dallas, Texas, at the annual meeting of the Southern Baptist Women in Ministry.

NOTES

1. Dorothee Sölle, *The Strength of the Weak* (Philadelphia: Westminster, 1984), 26.

2. Leszek Kolakowski, *Presentness of Myth* (Chicago: University of Chicago Press, 1989), 24.

3. Frederick Buechner, *Wishful Thinking: A Theological ABC* (New York, Harper & Row Publishers, 1973), 15.

4. John Robinson in *The Body* (Philadelphia: Westminster, 1952), 83.

5. Tertullian, *Apology.* 39.7.

6. Arthur Chute McGill, *Suffering: A Test of Theological Method* (Philadelphia: Westminster, 1982), 93.

We Preach Not Ourselves

2 Corinthians 4:5

Jan Fuller Carruthers

Part 1: We Have Nothing to Say

Just before the big meeting they were sitting at table, having supped together, and one of them leaned closer and said, "Teach us to preach." And he answered them with a parable:

"A certain minister was invited to preach at the national meeting. Long in advance she read and reread the passage, pondering its meanings. She pored over the text in the original language, compiled an outline of scriptural and spiritual truths to include in her sermon, consulted the concordance for final checks on significant word usages. She prayed for inspiration. Then she sat down with a pen and a legal pad. Long minutes passed, the sun went behind a cloud, and she wept. 'Dear God,' she cried, 'After all, I have nothing to say.'"

Then the disciples marveled among themselves because he spoke as one with authority, and yet they did not understand.

We have nothing to say. It's a periodic, painful, and regular lesson we learn as ministers of Christ. When we face the spiritual silence after the background work is done, we fear the worst. When our claims to intellectual acuity, to poetic empathy, to theological rightness and spiritual profundity are silenced, we find ourselves faced with the truth that *we have nothing to say.*

The human condition is one of emptiness; we spend our whole lives trying to convince ourselves that we have substance; that we are in control; that we have something important to say to the world; that the world needs us; that the world owes us a hearing; that God needs us and owes us our lives, our salvation, our safety, our place in the dominion of God. We pace our lives to prove that we are important and indispensable, avoiding the uncomfortable word that *we have nothing to say.*

We have nothing to say. Sometimes Scripture echoes the experiences of strangers to us. We do not recall the feelings, the events. We are not them and this is not the same road we travel; we do not recognize anything. Our silence is the answer to our dislocation. Other times, if the truth be known—and it will be—much of the time we do not understand this journey anyway. How can we speak in a strange language? These are not our words; I do not understand them. And when we think we understand what the life of faith and service is about, we are again proven ignorant or of little faith. Let's face it, we don't always want to understand either. Do we? And there are times when to understand is to wish we didn't? The silence in us swells loudly.

Often we have nothing to say in the face of faithful men and women of Scripture and history. Their impossible faith cows us into silence, and our lack of faith speaks for itself. (Paul always intimidates me this way.) We look away, numbly, almost resentful of their faithfulness, of their ability to accept emptiness with grace, and we wonder why we might have been called in the first place. We dare not preach ourselves.

That we have nothing to say is the beginning of the knowledge that there is a Reality far larger and more powerful than we are. To trust only our limited and empirical experience is to deny that Reality when we accept at the deepest level—and I'm not referring to intellectual assent or bandwagon agreement—if we experience the void deeply and see through it to the Presence on the other side, we can choose to become servants of that very real Presence. We are earthen, fragile vessels for this treasure of nothingness that is ultimately fullness.

We are *empty* vessels, earthy, earthen, and common. We have no corner on the truth. Christ does not belong to us. God is not a man or a woman; God is not even a Southern Baptist. We are voluntary slaves of Christ; we have handed away control so as not to fill ourselves with pretenses of being full. Our own words are empty, as are we; we have no credentials; we have nothing to say.

Having nothing to say shatters the illusion of our having any idea what this great mystery of God is essentially about, or of our having the words by which to adequately express it. Who among us knows the mind of God? But this may not necessarily lead to silence. We all know that from time to time we indulge ourselves in the fantasy of having something to say. And we all know someone who continues to speak in empty, meaningless words, even though we know they have nothing to say. On the other hand, there are great words to be spoken, but they are not ours. When we admit to emptiness and to being tongue-tied, we get out of the way for God to speak a Word. Now, if we preach, we preach Christ's truth, his gospel, his love and salvation. None of these are ours—they are the gifts, the substance for the empty vessels.

Knowing that we have nothing to say and are essentially unable to say it, we are free. We are free to depend on the One who has and shares with us something worth saying. We experience dependency— painful dependency—servanthood and *the gift*. Servanthood frees us from having to protect ourselves from knowing the truth about this self and other selves. We release our expectations to be brilliant and thoughtful, witty and wise, and now we speak the truth without regard for craftiness or cunning that woos people to listen, or we remake the truth so that it is palatable for those we want to impress. In order to be free, we must be empty. Did you ever play tunes with a stick and bottles filled with various levels of water? The full bottle makes a tinny, shallow, restless melody. The empty bottle echoes the richest, deepest sound. There is room for vibration and sound waves and tones. Our proclamation must be without hindrance—free and true.

Our confession of true emptiness and wordlessness, that we dare not preach ourselves (better we have nothing to say) frees us to say something useful. Now we are free to speak those words that are not our own. And so, shall we speak?

Part 2: We Have a Song: We Preach Christ As Lord

There is in New Haven a very talented musician, Dorothy Barn- hart, with whom I have had the great privilege of studying singing. After a recent lesson I asked her, "How is it that you teach people to sing? What do you do, and why?"

"Anyone can sing," she answered. "Everyone has a voice to use. The body is the instrument; anyone can learn to use it properly if they want to. People try so hard to sing. They tense, they push the sound; they work at it. The sound knows what to do. The song knows how to sing. I teach people to trust the song and to get out of the way. It takes a lot of hard work to learn what is in the way, and how to get it out of the way. And it takes practice, practice, practice. But when a song is free, you'll know it—because it will absolutely ring for you!" Could it be that we are learning to sing from silence to singing? We try hard to preach. We tense, we push the words: we work at it. We have nothing to say, and so we get out of the way. Now we have a song to sing. Now we are beginning to be free to sing a song that is not our own.

We are vessels of a song. Vessels. Beautiful vessels, at once common and uncommon and no doubt costly. We are empty containers, not glamorous, not flashy or showy, just useful when the Master determines for us to be useful. It is not even our life contained in the vessel. It is *the life,* the spiritual life of Christ, the true life we are fortunate and gifted to share.

We are privileged and honored. This treasure in our hearts operates in us, as well as in all its superlative greatness, from us as ministers, upon others, to bless them also with salvation. We cannot produce the living power, we cannot control it, we can't really direct it. Sometimes we find it difficult even to feel blessed by it. But we are empty, willing recipients of it, for Christ's sake, containers from which the wine of new life is poured and shared.

The great power of God ought to be contained in priceless containers, not in fragile sorts such as we. We bump and break too easily. We are not strong, or airtight, or worthy of such a content. We are free to share in the priceless treasure, and we are free to suffer having faced the pain of having nothing to say. But is there anything more painful than acknowledging our very own emptiness?

We are fragile people, and we do not want to suffer. I believe that God does not want us to fall upon affliction. Paul makes it clear, seconded by our own experience, that the earnest follower of Christ may expect to be rejected, abused, abased, and beaten up. Will we not break at once under this attack? Even now some of us are at the point of falling apart. But search your experience and find inexplicable moments of calm, reason, and even faith. How would we survive if not by God's strength, by God's own call, and God's own power? Apart from some power outside ourselves, we would have long been destroyed in the fray. Paul manages to survive because he believes that death for a vessel does not destroy the life in it. Losing reminds us of the God who provides, the One for whose sake we serve, the One whom we preach. Paul can sing because his thankfulness exceeds his grief. Does yours? Will mine? God, can you teach even us to sing?

"We have this treasure in earthen vessels, to show that the transcendent power belongs to God and not to us" (2 Corinthians 4:7, RSV). God chooses vessels that are easily broken in order to keep the matter clear about from where and from whom comes the power to survive. We cannot do for ourselves, so we dare not preach ourselves. God's purpose is to demonstrate the greatness of divine power, uncompromised by humanity. And now we find ourselves back where we began: we have nothing to say and nothing to do. We are getting out of the way, but we are learning to sing a song.

Singing teaches us to be vessels of the songs of God. We are fragile vessels of a song that creates the melody as it winds itself through our lives. It will be of tenderness and calm, of endurance and hope, of anger and pain, of sadness and laughter, of emptiness and joy, and of love. A true song, a song of God.

We ministers of the Word have nothing to say, but now we have a song. And we will sing the song of Christ, of great thanksgiving, love and grace, the Word of all words, the Song of all songs. We learn to sing, to get out of the way so that the song may be true and free to sing of Christ as Lord.

To preach is to sing in tones clearly not our own but from deep inside us. To utter the words of God is to speak with a familiar accent words that are foreign to us. We have nothing of our own to say, but that which is given us we will gladly proclaim with our best voice—at times without really understanding why. We do not recognize the song, but we willingly stand and spin it forth from our hearts. Examine your hearts. Do you want to sing?

We sing a song of truth.

Nothing is as strong, as convincing, as sure, or as good as the truth. Truth needs no outside argument. Its mere presence is greater than all argument. Now we speak of this supreme and saving truth, the reality of the Word. If truth itself cannot win a conscience, what can you or I add to truth to make it win? Sing it clearly just as we know it. All victories of the truth are 100 percent its own.

In the final scene of Shakespeare's tragedy *King Lear,* corpses litter the stage—corpses of the good and bad, wise and foolish, weak and strong, all alike, all dead. Edgar stammers the final lines of the play:

> *The weight of this sad time we must obey,*
> *Speak what we feel, not what we ought to say.*
> *(5.3.324-325)*

Throughout the entire masterpiece, Shakespeare makes a statement less concerned with matters of form, clarity, and good taste than with simply telling the truth. When King Lear takes off his clothes and babbles seeming nonsense, we may wonder; but these are words which are most human and clear, with whom listeners identify most strongly in the work. There seems to be no risk that Shakespeare is not willing to run, as if from the conviction that, if the truth is worth telling, it is worth making a fool of yourself to tell. We sing a song of truth.

To tell the truth is to live the truth and to be willing to make a fool of yourself in order to do so. To live the truth is to let the ultimate reality pursue us—the reality that turns the world on its ear, that shows up the emptiness of it all, that makes most real what is unseen and eternal. Shall we sing it? Creator, teach us to sing the song of truth, and we will sing until the end.

We sing a song of sadness and hope.

Sadly enough in the face of this truth, we have nothing to say, and our emptiness weighs us heavily down. We are on the verge of losing what heart we have left. We do not find it easy to believe or to sing or to have faith or to follow. We are afflicted in every way, perplexed, persecuted, and struck down. But we are somehow still alive. We are neither crushed, driven to despair, forsaken, nor destroyed (2 Corinthians 4:8). Paul fiercely clung to his belief that he would not remember his afflictions and suffering in relation to the glory of meeting the Christ face-to-face. God, grant us such forgetfulness, grant us such faith in providence and eternity, grant that our thank-fulness will exceed our grief.

It is faith alone that allows us to say, "I believe even when afflicted, and so I speak." And so I sing. Faith in the God who raised Jesus from the dead reminds us not to fear death. Faith in the God who provides for the needs of the saints allows us to cast ourselves on God's mercy in the midst of our most painful moments. It is faith in the God of life—eternal and spiritual life—that enables us to see beyond the temporal life we know and the sufferings we feel to something even more real and more ultimate. And it is faith in the Redeemer God that allows us to give thanks before knowing the final outcome.

The word is that we do not lose heart. We may be discouraged and feel faint at the privileged call to serve God. We may not feel privileged at all. Hope hears and clings to the words of the prophet Isaiah, the word of the Lord:

> *Have you not known?*
> *Have you not heard?*
> *The LORD is the everlasting God,*
> *the Creator of the ends of the earth.*
> *[God] does not faint or grow weary;*
> *[God's] understanding is unsearchable.*
> *[God] gives power to the faint,*
> *and strengthens the powerless.*
> *Even youths will faint and be weary,*
> *and the young will fall exhausted;*
> *but those who wait for the LORD*
> *shall renew their strength,*
> *they shall mount up with wings like eagles,*
> *they shall run and not be weary,*
> *they shall walk and not faint.*
> *Isaiah 40:28-31*

To look with eyes of faith is to see a God who never faints and who will not let us lose heart. Shall we sing this song of endurance and faith? Redeemer God, teach us this song of sadness and hope, and we will sing it as we have breath.

We sing a song of thanksgiving.

We have nothing to say, and we are learning a song. We preach the gospel of Christ so that many may know God's grace, so that thanksgiving may increase. The new power of life we share in emptiness is grace-renewing, refreshing love of God for unworthies like we are. A song of thanksgiving? Here we may falter. We can sing the truth; we can sing pain and mean it. We can almost sing hope. But sometimes the melody seems thin at thanksgiving.

Dear sisters and brothers, the song is being sung. Vessels can carry this tune. Shall we join the hymn? Are we at once weak enough and strong enough to fall into the arms of God, to trust the song and to let it carry us to the heart of our Lord where the song ends and begins again. Can we get out of the way and sing for all we are worth before God? We cannot be silent, for this is where we all sing together.

Shall we sing this song of thanksgiving to God, for all our emptiness, for our silence and wordlessness, for fragility and power and sharing and depending and eternal living? Holy Spirit, teach us to sing the song of thanksgiving, and we will raise together an everlasting psalm to God's glory. All the songs you have taught us now wind in refrains of straining truth and tender pain, of brave endurance, calming hope, rested faith, and laughing joy. You sing through us, and we will sing with you until all of life becomes one great and eternal symphony of praise to Christ.

This sermon was preached in June 1986 at the annual meeting of the Southern Baptist Women in Ministry in Atlanta, Georgia.

Visions of a New Humanity

Luke 1:36-53

Lynda Weaver-Williams

We have an Advent text. You may think we're either six months early or six months late. But this is not a story to save for Christmas. Long before now you have found strength and encouragement in this wondrous woman named Mary. One of the fifteenth-century paintings of the Annunciation has Mary hearing the once-in-a-life-time news in a room just off a busy city street. Outside her window it's business as usual; the merchants trade, deals are made, an animal wanders by, a child peeps around the corner. But inside, it's only Mary, poised, leaning forward to hear a word from the Lord.

We are all Mary today, desiring to hear a word from God. Outside it's business as usual. But inside, it's only us, leaning forward, poised to hear a word from the Lord.

It happens every day. Pregnant women talk. Talk women talk. Talk baby talk. "I felt the baby move this morning." Eyeing each other growing round and heavy. In grocery check-out lines, in clinic waiting rooms, pregnant women talk, "When's yours due?" Common talk for an uncommon event.

And so it happened with Mary and Elizabeth. They talk women talk. And baby talk. And God talk. Because with Mary and Elizabeth, it's a whole new story. Their everyday circumstances, their uncommon event is of God—God's initiative, God's holy surprise. And nobody knows better than these two pregnant women.

This is a story of belief. "My spirit rejoices in God my Savior," sings Mary (Luke 1:46). And Elizabeth pronounces a blessing on Mary who believed, as Scripture says, that there would be a fulfillment of what was spoken to her from the Lord. From the Lord. No confusion here on the source of authority.

Blessed is she, says Elizabeth, because she believed her child was of God. If you're counting, as Raymond Brown has, it's the first blessing of the New Testament, and it's placed upon the shoulders of this poor, unwed teenager because she believed.

In one of his Advent sermons, Martin Luther found three miracles in the Virgin Birth: God became human, a virgin conceived, and Mary believed. For him, the last was the greatest.

And how extraordinary that she did believe! Jesus was surrounded his whole life by people who saw miracles yet were unbelieving; who heard his preaching and walked away unconvinced; who met the resurrected Lord and doubted. But Mary believed.

If [professor and theologian] Fred Craddock is right, and ignorance is the particular impediment to faith in Luke, then in this story Mary is twice blessed. She knew God's word when she heard it, and she believed in its fulfillment.

Not unlike us, who have heard God's word and call and know it for the clear, holy voice we believe it is. Amid choruses of protests, we believe. In spite of resolutions, accusations, and threats, we believe, as Mary, that there is—even in this moment—a fulfillment of what has been spoken to us of the Lord. Understand, here, that there is no question about our authority. None whatsoever. Our authority is from the Lord God, and none other. No board, no agency, no document.

You can believe that! Our story, like Mary before us, is one of belief.

But it's not enough. Not enough to know and believe. Not for Mary and not for us. What was it Mary said? Let it be to me, for I am the handmaid, the slave of the Lord. Beyond believing, Mary was obedient.

Now, obedience is a dusty old idea in our world—and in our church, too. In a *Time* cover story on ethics, one expert says it is just the neglect of a sense of duty—of obedience—that brought down the Wall Street brokerage firms as well as Jim and Tammy Bakker. Obedience is not much practiced. We'd rather talk of personhood than obedience.

But not for Mary. For her the bottom line is obedience, not self-actualization. Obedience to God, following the Christ who followed the cross. Doing what we must, against the grain, against our own logic, even against our own preferences.

One of the first women to be hanged in this country was Mary Dyer, who in 1669 was accused of being a Quaker and a prophetess. She was arrested, spent time in jail, and finally was banished from Boston for, as she said, "speaking the Words the Lord spoke to me." She returned to Boston and was finally sentenced to death. As she stood on the gallows, she was given a last chance to "repent." "Nay," she said, "I cannot, for in obedience to the will of God I came, and in his will I abide faithful unto death."[1]

Obedience, not blind submission. From endless congressional testimony we've heard about the damage that simply "following orders" can do. Obedience, not passive resignation. There is no virtue in going through the motions. Obedience—positive, active, faithful, eschatological obedience.

A Woman's Missionary Union friend of mine says she is often asked of this present crisis [in the Southern Baptist Convention], "What will women do?" In a matter-of-fact voice she says, "Women will do what we've always done. Women will be faithful and obedient."

And she's right. As always, women will bear witness and teach and preach and sing. Women will care for the children and the cast-offs. We'll run the shelters and feed the hungry. We'll be vigilant for missions and the spreading of the gospel. We'll dream and plan and watch and wait for the kingdom. We'll be obedient.

Not blindly or undiscerningly. But we will be obedient to speak or teach or sing or write the words the Lord has spoken to us. Because like Mary, without obedience, our response to God is not enough.

So here we are, dutiful daughters. What we were raised to be. And here we all are, dutiful, obliging.

But that's not why we're here. That's not what this is about. If Mary were merely obliging God's presence in her body, we wouldn't even have this story. And if dutiful daughters were all we were, then we'd not even go to the considerable trouble it takes to be here.

How many back flips did you do in order to arrange to be here this weekend? We drove eight hours to the grandparents with our two- and seven-year-old sons so that the children could be cared for. That's eight hours in the opposite direction from St. Louis. Now, my sense of "duty" dropped off after about the first hour of the trip.

No, it's not duty that brings us here. This is not duty; this is worship. This is more than obligation; this is extravagance. We haven't come all this way to meet requirements of duty. We are here to overflow in praise, to worship without apology or reservation the God who has called us.

Theologian and preacher George Buttrick told of a writer whose words impressed him. "I want to worship God for no reason at all." We want to worship today simply because it is in us to do so. No explanations. No qualifications.

Now, we should be honest: there is no reasonable call to praise. Ask around. On that our friends, foes, the press, everyone can agree. We Baptist women in ministry have no reasonable call to praise. Hanging between two cliffs of this denominational chasm, sometimes not being able to tell one side from the other, there is no reasonable call to praise.

Our own heritage snatched away, our mother church abandoning us, our memories of Girl's Auxiliary faithfulness, our youth camp commitments, marred by broken promises. There is no reasonable call to praise.

Like Mary, we are unclaimed, unheeded, unbelieved, unwelcomed; so let's do something uncalled for! Let's sing and praise and testify to the greatness of God Almighty.

No reasonable call to praise? Then we shall. Indeed we shall. Let's raise the rafters in telling the greatness of God. For there is nothing more powerful or radical we can do this morning than to worship here among the unofficial, unendorsed, unordained.

So sing, dutiful daughters! Praise, obedient sons! Let all that is within you bless God's holy name!

For we are signs of the kingdom, you and I. Not images or reflections, but actual living signs announcing the early arrival of the kingdom of God, that very kingdom to which Isaiah says a child shall lead us. Where the wolf and the lamb are no longer enemies. Where, as Mary sings, the hungry get bushel baskets of food and the poor are picked up and carried. And where the big boys, as civil rights activist and author Clarence Jordan calls them, have their thrones and plexiglass podiums swept away in the imaginations of their hearts by the strong arm of the Lord. That's the kingdom we announce here and now with our lives. And while we await its fullness, we are the signs of the kingdom.

Now, that's hard for you to buy, isn't it? Us, signs of the kingdom? We can call upon sisters of faith through the ages who were signs: nineteenth-century Baptist missionaries Lottie Moon and Annie Armstrong, Deborah and Phoebe, Mother Teresa and Sojourner Truth. But me? I can't even find a job. A sign of the Kingdom?

I am the daughter of nobody you ever heard of, raised in a church you don't know, from a town with which you are unfamiliar. There is nothing to commend me to the gospel ministry except that the Lord God has called me. Only in God's kingdom could my life have happened as it has. Only as signs of the kingdom do our lives make sense. We need only have eyes to see.

Mary saw that reality. Within her own body she felt what God was doing in her life. But she raised her eyes to see that God was doing the same thing in the world: giving birth to a new order. The birth of God's kingdom is not an easy birth. It is prolonged and painful. But its joyful fulfillment is assured. And we are its signs.

My husband, who is becoming a seasoned observer of women in ministry, says that one of the best things we have going for us is that we're women. That may seem obvious, but sometimes I think we forget. We're women. And that means we have a unique perspective because of the way God made us, the way we were raised, and the way we live our lives. That perspective is particularly true in this story.

Being pregnant is a real education. Mary could testify to that, and some of us could, too. The child inside you grows and moves on its own, living by its own schedule, even arriving in its own time. And you realize, "Here is something within me, but I do not possess it nor control it." For mothers and disciples everywhere, that should be a welcome word. The world, the church, the children, the kingdom does not rest on my shoulders alone. I can let go of some of that overwhelming control.

Perhaps as much as anything we need to hear about letting go. Poised to hear a word from the Lord, we have heard of Mary's belief and obedience and praise. Mary was also the disciple and mother who later let go of her son in faith.

David Buttrick, of Vanderbilt Divinity School, tells of a minister in the North who papered a wall in her church office. The custom-made wallpaper repeats words, line after line, all over the wall. So now she can sit at her desk and read the repeated reminder, "Trust God, let go. Let go, trust God."

We are signs of the kingdom. We needn't hold on so tight, grasping at grace that is already ours. I think Mary would agree with the twentieth-century wallpaper words, "Trust God, let go." Just let go, sisters and brothers, and trust God.

This sermon was preached in St. Louis, Missouri, at the annual meeting of the Southern Baptist Women in Ministry in June 1987.

Reprinted by permission from *Amidst Babel, Speak the Truth: Reflections on the Southern Baptist Convention Struggle,* ed. Robert U. Ferguson, Jr. (Greenville, S. C.: Smith & Helwys, 1993).

NOTES

1. Rosemary R. Reuther, Rosemary Skinner Keller, eds., *Women in Religion in America* (New York: Harper & Row, 1983), 28.

Prophesy by Faith

1 Corinthians 12:4-7; Romans 12:6-8

Jann Aldredge-Clanton

The first time I went to the ordination of a woman, I was curious. I just wanted to know what a woman minister was like; I didn't want to be one. I didn't want to risk disapproval. Growing up I was so shy that I would do almost anything to keep from speaking before a group. Once I almost refused an opportunity to go to Glorieta Baptist Assembly because I knew that I would have to report to the church when I came back. But here I stand before you—a woman minister, in a prophetic role.

All of us here this morning are prophets. We are prophets because we can imagine what is yet to be. I come today with a vision. You come with a vision. We all come with prophetic visions. I envision the day when Southern Baptists recognize that God distributes gifts according to grace, not gender. When women and men stand side by side in ministry, including the pastorate. When we see women and men serving equally on all our boards and agencies. When we can go to Southern Baptist Convention meetings and thrill to the rich harmony of male and female voices from the pulpit as well as the choir. When we can open a state Baptist newspaper and see pictures of women as well as men, and read stories of women using their gifts in Christ's ministry. When we can walk into any Southern Baptist church and be greeted by deacons, female and male, black and white. When we teach our girls that they are just as truly in the image of God as boys.

Our prophetic imaginations compel us to gather here today to act out our visions. The prophetic tradition in Scripture goes beyond preaching to include actions that proclaim God's truth as challenge to the prevailing culture. We gather here today as clergywomen unrecognized by the Southern Baptist Convention. We gather here today as laymen and laywomen supportive of women in ministry, perhaps ostracized because of going against the flow of Southern Baptist culture. Our very presence here places us in a prophetic role. We here today have a variety of gifts. But we share the gift of prophecy. A prophet goes out ahead and shows the way even when the way may be difficult or dangerous. Perhaps we feel uncomfortable with this prophetic gift. Maybe we feel frightened by it. The crucial issue is whether or not we claim this gift of prophecy and exercise it by faith.

We live in a critical time in the history of our denomination; the need for prophetic leadership urgent and compelling. In the latter part of the eighteenth century, the founders of our country saw themselves as shapers of the future and accepted this role with energy and optimism. During this period Abigail Adams wrote, "Great necessities call forth great leaders." In the Southern Baptist Convention, we hear cries of great necessities on every hand. One group cries the necessity of power in the hands of only those who agree with their version of biblical inspiration and their political agenda. Another group cries the necessity of return to the "good ol' days" of the priesthood of the believer, which in reality was the priesthood of only male believers. God has called and equipped us to proclaim the necessity of a new vision.

Our denomination desperately needs leaders who will speak in a different voice, a voice that affirms the gifts of all God's children, a voice that proclaims liberty for the oppressed, a voice that is indeed good news to the poor, a voice that calls for servant not authoritarian leaders, a voice of cooperation not competition in ministry, a voice of peace not of war. We can slip into the background and deny our gift, deny our distinctive voice in the Southern Baptist Convention and the history of Christianity. Or we can seize this present crucial moment to proclaim God's transforming truth. It takes faith to speak in a different voice. By faith let us prophesy a new vision.

I have a friend who will not come to local Women in Ministry meetings because she says they make our gender too much of an issue. She protests, "I am a minister, not a woman minister!" We all long for the day when "minister" equally designates female and male. But we are not there yet. At this point our very presence as ministers is prophecy. The very existence of Southern Baptist Women in Ministry is prophecy—a challenge to male domination. By claiming who we are, by claiming our distinctive place in history as women ministers, we can break down walls of patriarchal religion. To do this we need to connect with one another in groups that nurture and empower us. We must not stop with prophesying within our own groups; we must challenge unethical, stifling sexism within our entire denomination. We must not stop with tearing down this evil in the church; we must speak out against sexism throughout our society. We must not stop with challenging the system; we must act courageously to create a new order of justice and cooperative leadership. If we do church the way males have always done it, then we squander our unique gifts and limit the Spirit within us.

A friend of mine gave as her reason for ordination, "We must have power to give it away." The authors of *The Feminization of America* see women's skills of cooperation and mutuality as positively influencing our entire country. The word of hope is that women's growing influence in the public world brings a new social consciousness and a more compassionate society. To be the redemptive body of Christ, the church needs our feminization of administration, preaching, education, pastoral counseling, and all varieties of ministry.

Sisters and empathic brothers, we hold in our hands the keys to a faith community that values the gifts of every member. God has placed us in the Southern Baptist Convention for such a time as this. God calls us to proclaim and live out the truth that gifts are conferred according to the grace of God, not the whim of a convention resolution nor of any Baptist association's action. God calls us to celebrate the varieties of gifts and the varieties of service and the varieties of working. Since it is the same God who inspires each gift, each gift is precious, worthy of our respect and nurture.

We hold in our hands the keys to a community that models inclusiveness of gender and race, not just for fairness but for the enrichment that comes with diverse gifts. The gifts of female and male, black and brown and white are all manifestations of the Spirit for the common good. Hierarchies and segregations quench the Spirit. Inclusive communities with servant leaders manifest the Spirit for the enrichment of all.

It takes faith to build these new communities. By faith let us imagine these communities. What we see in our minds can become reality. By faith let us preach these visions. By faith let us act out these visions. By our thoughts and prayers and words and actions of faith, let us prophesy these new communities into existence.

God calls us to prophesy, whatever form our ministry takes according to our grace gifts. Gifts come to us by grace. Using them takes faith. Prophecy especially requires faith. According to Romans 12, our prophecy is in "proportion to our faith." It is ironic that some interpreters have used this phrase to eliminate those with whom they did not agree. By taking "faith" to mean a dogmatic creed, they attempted to use ecclesiastical authority to silence prophets. To advance conformity and dogmatism, they distorted a text that admonishes free exercise of a diversity of gifts.

Those in power in our convention seek to stifle the gifts of women. By an ecclesiastical authority foreign to Scripture and our Baptist heritage, they think they can silence the prophecy of daughters. Our denomination, which once encouraged us to develop our gifts and to go wherever God leads now, now tells us we cannot go into the pulpit. Because we are women, we are unacceptable as preachers. Because we are women, we are unacceptable as deacons. We are unacceptable to perform baptism, to serve the Lord's Supper.

With these messages pounding in our ears, what keeps us going? What keeps us holding on? Faith, my sisters and brothers, faith—the assurance of things hoped for, the conviction of things not seen, the commitment to things not seen, the holding on and keeping on even in the darkness. Our prophecy depends on our faith in the vision God has burned deep within our souls, not on any convention or board or agency. Either we are limited by lack of faith, or we are unleashed by our faith to bold words and deeds.

Winston Churchill once gave the commencement address to a Harvard graduating class. He arose on the auspicious occasion and said to the graduates, "Never, never, never give up!" And then he sat down. To all of us here today, I say, "Have faith. Never, never, never give up!"

Baptist foremothers have led the way. Eunice Marshall did not give up. She suffered imprisonment because she would not stop preaching.[1] Martha Marshall, on trial for religious dissent, preached a sermon so powerful that it convicted most of the jury of their need to repent.[2] Twenty-three-year-old Lucinda Williams had enough faith to start the first Baptist church in a town so hostile to Baptists that three Baptist churches had already failed. Though people tried to discourage her, she would not give up. This church, founded by Lucinda Williams, grew to be the largest Southern Baptist church in the world—First Baptist Church of Dallas, Texas.[3] We need the faith of our foremothers to found churches that model racial and gender inclusiveness, mutual instead of hierarchical leadership. By faith we can found these churches even in a hostile environment. By faith let us prophesy these churches into existence.

Such faith is risky business. But burying our gifts means death. The gift of prophecy will die if we bury it. If we try to preserve safety, to avoid risk, then God's gift dies within us. In his interpretation of the parable of the talents, author Dan Via sees the fear of the one-talent servant as the anxiety of a person who will not step into the unknown. This servant acted as little as possible, hoping for a safe bargain. It takes risk to fulfill God-given possibilities. Self-protective nonaction leads to darkness and death.

If we sit around waiting for the convention to pass a resolution approving ordination of women, our unique gifts will waste away. Prophetic leadership is not delegated. It is assumed. Amos did not wait for the religious authorities of his day to vote their approval of his message of justice for the poor and oppressed. Authorized by God alone, he assumed the prophetic role. Esther did not receive the golden scepter of approval before her prophetic action on behalf of her people. Upheld by her faith community, she took the prophetic risk. We cannot wait for official authorization or approval. Our message is too urgent. Our gifts are too precious. Our vision is too compelling. We can defer our dream no longer. Poet Langston Hughes asks the question,

> *What happens to a dream deferred?*
> *Does it dry up*
> *like a raisin in the sun?*
> *Or fester like a sore—*
> *And then run?*
> *Does it stink like rotten meat?*

Or crust and sugar over—
like a syrupy sweet?
Maybe it just sags
like a heavy load.
Or does it explode?[4]

We can defer our dream no longer. By faith we must prophesy our dream into reality.

Such risky faith can be lonely and scary. Eighteen-year-old Tania Aebi set out in her twenty-six-foot sailboat with a dream. She dreamed of becoming one of the youngest people ever to sail around the world alone. She tells of a frightening time out in a storm. "Suddenly the boat lurched, flipped on its side, and my world turned upside down. Oh my God, what to do? Through the lightning, I realized I was in the hold of a full-fledged tempest. I was in dire straits. I swore I never wanted to see this miserable ocean again. I prayed, 'Please, God, I've had it. Please, please give me a break. I can't take anymore.'" In the course of her journey, Tania had met a friend who was also sailing around the world. Tania says what got her through this stormy time and others was knowing that her friend was out on the ocean going through the same thing. "To have a friend sailing on the same ocean and with the same destination gave me such courage and strength. I always had the feeling that, come what may, someone dear to me was living through it with me. To arrive in a foreign port and know that my friend would already be there or would arrive soon, would make me feel connected and less alone."[5]

Today we are setting out together. We are launching out on the same faith venture together. We are setting forth to use our differing grace-gifts to prophesy by faith. Whether through social ministries or music or education or giving or pastoral care or preaching, we can prophesy. Stormy times lie ahead. Lonely times lie ahead. When we are far from the security of this place and we feel we are all alone, remember there are friends out there in the same storm with the same destination. When we are tired and scared and feel we can't take anymore, remember we are out on the stormy sea together. Sisters and brothers, remember and take faith and courage.

Most importantly, we can be certain that no matter how far away from security and approval, Christ will never leave us nor forsake us.

Christ goes with us. We are not alone. Christ who inspires us to launch
out sails on the same ocean. Our most faithful Friend lives through
the storms with us and calls us, saying, "Take courage. Be not afraid.
Daughters and sons of God, arise. Launch out together. By faith
prophesy."

*This sermon was preached in June 1988 in San Antonio, Texas, at the
annual meeting of the Southern Baptist Women in Ministry.*

NOTES

1. Leon McBeth, *Women in Baptist Life* (Nashville: Broadman Press, 1979),
101-102.

2. James Donovan Mosteller, *History of Kiokee Baptist Church in Georgia* (Ann
Arbor, Mich.: Edwards Brothers Press, 1952), 130-131.

3. William L. Lumpkin, *Baptist Foundations in the South* (Nashville: Broadman
Press, 1961), 23.

4. Langston Hughes, "Dream Deferred" from *The Panther and the Lash* (New
York: Alfred A. Knopf, Inc., 1951).

5. *Cruising World,* November 1987, 65-69.

Becoming Community

Ephesians 4

Betty Winstead McGary

Christmas 1987 was very special for my extended family. My parents always hosted our annual family gathering at their home in Louisville, Kentucky. But Christmas 1987 was different: their children, grandchildren, and great-grandchildren were all together for the first time in ten years.

This annual event started over thirty years ago. When my three children and my brother's four daughters were small, we all spent many happy Christmases together. Two young couples, seven children, and their grandparents shared presents, attended Christmas Eve service, and had Christmas dinner with a host of other relatives and friends on Christmas Day. It was the ideal family scene.

About our hosts. My parents grew up Southern Baptist in small towns in western Kentucky. They moved to Louisville as young adults, met, and married fifty-six years ago in the midst of the Great Depression. There are many ways I could describe them, but I choose one word: loyal. They are loyal to God, to each other, their family, friends, church, country, political party, the Dodgers, and the Ford Motor Company. Over long careers they were loyal to Capitol Holding Company, where Dad was an executive, and the Jefferson County Public Schools, where Mom was an educator. They lived the Protestant work ethic. There was no confusion with them. There were no identity crises. Values were clear.

Their annual Christmas reunion is symbolic of who they are and what they care about. Each year we look forward to it and all it teaches us about our roots and our progress.

As the grandchildren grew up, great changes occurred in the lives of our family members. For many years it wasn't possible for everyone to come to the party. So we were excited to be back together again this Christmas. But the scene had changed. My brother's former wife was there. I was alone. My brother's oldest daughter is now Memerie Nuramundrad. Her husband came to America from Iran ten years ago. He introduced Mem's sister, Kelli, to his friend, Emir. They are married and came to the party with their children, Katy and Bryce. Another sister, Tracey, came with her husband, Jay. They are young professionals and Presbyterians. Robin, the youngest, brought her fiancé, Bob. She had joined the Catholic church where they plan to be married.

My three children were there. They once described themselves as "a hippie, a preppie, and a normal." Tom, the oldest, was a college theater major. He played in a band called "Average Life," and supported causes such as civil rights, and end to apartheid, and world peace. He brought his girlfriend, Alyson, an artist and recent college graduate who liked fashion and hoped to climb the corporate ladder. Andrew, a responsible college student, brought Jill, who looked like an angel.

We were an interesting group—with little in common, you could say. But we have two hours of video tape that attest to all the laughter and love we shared that day. On Christmas Eve, the den was piled halfway to the ceiling with presents. We put three-month-old Ashley Nuramundrad, the youngest great-grandchild, on a white lace pillow on the pile of gifts for videos and photographs. She delighted us with her smiles.

It couldn't have been more appropriate for this group: Dad called on his daughter, the minister, to bless the meal. I was flooded with memories and emotions as the group fell silent. Above all, I was filled with gratitude for Mom and Dad, who loved each one of us, shared our struggles, prayed for us, and invited us to come to the party. They reminded me of the love of God. It is God's love that enables us to transform our relationships into real community.

Becoming community is challenge, even in the family. In Ephesians 4, Paul says that through Jesus Christ we have a way to unity. He appeals to his readers to live lives worthy of the high calling to which they are called, which can be paraphrased "the place for which God has appointed you in all the ages." Christians are to serve together in relation to God's design of universal unity

In verses 1-6, Paul says that Christ has given each of his followers distinctive spiritual gifts so that each may make his or her particular contribution to the good of the whole. He also says in verses 14-16 that the ability to achieve unity is the mark of maturity. As a student of adult faith development, I've been excited by the work of James Fowler, who wrote *Becoming Adult, Becoming Christian,*[1] and others whose research has identified stages of faith development. Fowler says that our images of the good man or woman are in ferment. In answer to the question, "What is maturity?" he says spiritually mature people are those who are ever widening their circle of love, those who see the world through the eyes of God. After years of research on people's lives, Fowler contends that wholeness, maturity, and excellence of being come as by-products and resultant virtues of the lives of those who are falling in love with the One who intends, and is bringing, a universal commonwealth of love. The spiritually mature, he says, are partners with God in creation, in governing, and in freedom and redemption. This is essentially what Paul says in Ephesians 4.

Achieving community is costly. There are barriers to community. We fail to become community from *lack of effort*. Becoming community is demanding. It requires effort to actively listen to others, to hear and internalize their stories, to see the world through their eyes. It takes effort to become self-aware, to risk our illusions by facing reality, and to share ourselves without giving ourselves away. We fail at becoming community when we don't work at it.

Another barrier to community is *the desire for sameness and predictability*. Becoming community involves a process of changing and being changed. To open ourselves to new ideas and to new dimensions in relationships requires a constant process of letting go that can be both painful and exciting. Maintaining predictability and sameness is a way we try to avoid pain and growth. It's also a way we miss the power of God in our lives.

I believe the greatest barrier to community is *the need to dominate and control*. Deep within us lurks the fear that there is not enough and that we must compete and control to assure that our place will be secure and our needs met. This happens in relationships. Love is snuffed out by dependency. We make alliances of weakness rather than strength. It happens in families that become so enmeshed that members no longer have choices. It is happening in our denomination. Against our great heritage as champions of religious freedom, one group has decided that they know what is best for all of us and that their agenda, when accepted by all, will lead to the betterment of our whole society.

I believe that the need to control is rooted in faithlessness. To believe that my truth is all the truth there is—that my perceptions, my needs, my experiences are ultimate reality—leaves God out of the process and denies the work of the Holy Spirit. Our spouses, our children, our friends, members of our communities, our churches, and our larger family of faith are not foes to be conquered and not possessions to be used. They too, like us, are God's children, our sisters, our brothers. We are not called to control each other; we are called to be faithful to each other and to God.

How do we become community? It is tempting to believe that the way to belong is to be all things to all people. Without identity, boundaries, and self-awareness, there is fusion, but this is not community. In Ephesians 4, Paul makes clear that the unity of the church does not consist of uniformity, with the suppression of individual gifts, but each believer makes his or her own contribution to the whole.

A major task in the development of any individual is that of *defining the self.* This involves differentiating oneself from the family of origin and discovering personal needs, wants, desires, capabilities, and calling. It involves paying the price to become. We cannot share ourselves if we have not a self to give.

Community requires *relationship and respect for others.* This is called intimacy. Intimacy is somewhere between closeness and distance; but as Henri Nouwen reminds us, intimacy is not halfway between the two.[2] There is always the space, and it can leave us breathless at times. Dietrich Bonhoeffer, in his classic work *Life Together,* says that Christ is in the space listening to each one, knowing each heart, drawing us together and to God. With Christ in the space that is between us, the miracle of intimacy can happen.

The message of the gospel is that *there is no identity without community.* We need each other; we need to be interdependent. It is important to notice in Ephesians that the gifts of grace are said to be the gifts of Christ, "according to the measure of Christ's gift" (Ephesians 4:7). The phrase suggests limitations upon the gifts for service accorded to any one individual; the gifts of each need to be supplemented by the gifts of all that we may all attain "to the measure of the full stature of Christ" (Ephesians 4:13). We are created for community. Cooperation is woven into God's design for the world. As we discover God's reality, we can "let go" of our need to control and compete. We can remove ourselves from the tyranny of time, with its demand that we achieve our destiny before it's too late. In Jesus Christ we can develop our gifts, share them in community, and bear fruits that will last through time and eternity. Every stage of life becomes a stage of growth, and in death we will say, "the best is yet to be."

Modern humanity has cherished the illusion that becoming community is relatively easy. We often think that all we need to do is bring people together, get them to communicate with each other, and the deed is done. Our naïve assumption has been that in leagues of nations, councils of churches, and other groupings in conference halls, seminars, and discussion groups, community will happen. But the truth is, the closer we come together, and the better we communicate, the greater may be our awareness of mutual faults and intolerable differences.

Does the history of Christianity still testify to an underlying unity in the midst of the sad story of the broken body of Christ? The answer is clearly yes. All Christians of whatever name still worship the same God. We unite in confessing Jesus as Lord. We share one hope of salvation. The Holy Spirit is still present whether we worship in a liturgical mass, a Greek Orthodox Eucharist, in the silence of a Quaker assembly, or an evangelistic service, or a Baptist church.

The true church is a great miracle. Becoming community requires grace. Each of us is by nature a little god to himself or herself. The church universal is a fellowship of repentant and forgiven sinners. Repentance is a kind of dying. Forgiveness means rising again. The church is a community of the dead and risen—that is what we are. Only such a community as ours dare speak of unity. Only such a fellowship can risk true togetherness.[3]

In the Crucifixion account in Matthew 27:51, we read, "The curtain of the temple was torn in two, from top to bottom." That curtain covered the Holy of Holies; it was the veil beyond which only the high priest could go on the Day of Atonement. The torn curtain is a symbol that God is not hidden and remote and that in the life and death of Jesus the way to God is now open to us all.

I love to imagine God as the conductor of a great choir and orchestra, with all humankind as its members. God is calling us each and all to sing the song, to play our notes, to join in the one "Hallelujah Chorus" that will never end. We are all gifted; we are all needed; we are all invited to lift our voices in the song.

This sermon was preached in January 1988 in Houston, Texas, at South Main Baptist Church.

NOTES

1. James Fowler, *Becoming Adult, Becoming Christian* (New York: Harper & Row, 1984).

2. Henri Nouwen, *Lifesigns* (New York: Doubleday, 1986).

3. Buttrick, *Interpreter's Bible X* (New York: Abingdon Press, 1953).

Too Good to Be True

Genesis 1:1-2; Luke 24:36-41a

Virginia C. Barfield

The story that we are told in the twenty-fourth chapter of Luke is not very difficult to grasp. The images are clear. The scene is nakedly real. Picture it with me:

1. On the morning of the first day of the week, women have come to the tomb to complete the burial rites. They meet angels, find that the body of their friend, master, Lord is missing. They are told not to worry and to pass this news on to the disciples: "Jesus is risen. Go to Galilee, and he'll meet you there."

2. Two of the disciples, the same day, on the road to Emmaus, meet Jesus but don't recognize him. Jesus explains the Scriptures to them. They eat together and, as Jesus breaks the bread, they suddenly figure out who he is and he disappears.

3. Total confusion occurs. The stories are overwhelming. The events of the past few days are just too much to deal with. The two disciples return to Jerusalem to tell the others what has been going on.

4. The confused, disheartened, doubting disciples gather together to convince themselves that the message the women proclaimed is really true. Jesus comes into their midst. He shows them his hands and feet, visible and tangible proof that the news is true, that order has come from chaos. They think that they are seeing a ghost! Jesus wants to convince them otherwise. They still cannot believe it. It is just too good to be true!

Is it hard to understand why these people could not believe the news that Jesus was indeed raised from the dead? Is it so hard for us to understand why these people were so disillusioned by the events of those horrible days? Is it hard to understand that Caiaphas, Pilate, and the "Good Friday" crowd had no real reason to believe that God was the author of good things? Could they be expected to respond in any way other than the way they did? Is it so strange that these disciples had to rub their eyes and look again to see if what was before them was really there? After all, chaos, confusion, doubt, disillusionment do have a way of begetting cynicism and disbelief—even in our lives today. They were still unconvinced, for it seemed too good to be true!

One of the most disheartening times of the day can be the hour spent watching the evening news. Reports of crime precede news of economic decline. Crackdowns on drug trafficking are in the spotlight at home, while political instability is highlighted abroad. Scientists work furiously to solve the mysteries of AIDS. Children starve to death at our doorsteps. A professional basketball player signs a $30 million contract, but there is no permanent shelter for the homeless in our city. A pregnant, unwed teenager jumps from an eighteenth-floor window. A grandmother worries that her pension is about to be cut—again. A freak car accident claims the life of a twenty-four-year-old father of two. Nuclear proliferation threatens the lives of us all. All in all, watching the news can be a pretty depressing way to find out what is going on in the world!

And not only are we confronted daily with the turmoil of the world at large, but we must also deal with personal pains and frustrations, with our private worlds of chaos and disillusion. At times, my life and yours can only be described as "chaotic." Maybe it's only minor problems that add up and make for a rotten day. You know the days when everything little goes wrong at once: the alarm malfunctions and we start the day behind schedule; we can't find a clean shirt or blouse that matches anything in the closet; the milk on the cereal is spoiled and there isn't another carton in the refrigerator; the battery in the car is dead. Any one of these by itself is only a minor irritation. But, put them all together in the span of an hour, and the result is chaos.

Then there are times when the pain and turmoil strike deeper than these trivial problems. A serious illness threatens our life or the life of someone we love; death separates us from a lifelong companion or spouse; hurt and intense pain spring from a relationship that has turned sour and has no future; heartbreak and disorientation result from dreams and ambitions shattered by circumstances beyond our control. All of us here today have experienced levels of deep and abiding pain and turmoil in our lives. All of us have known moments of real chaos. Some of us are even now experiencing a time of personal crisis and chaos. The pains are real and deep.

As we proclaim today the message of the gospel—the Good News that God is the author of good things, that evil can be dislodged by good, that order can be brought from chaos—it is not so strange that we respond with words similar to those in Luke: We can hardly believe the message of faith—it does seem too good to be true.

The verses that were read from Genesis—the introduction to the Creation account—tell about a time when God began the activity of shaping the world. Prior to the Creation event, the Scriptures tell us that all was formless and meaningless. Shape, solidarity, and structure were lacking. All was waste and void. Yet God's spirit was moving, even then, over the emptiness and chaos. God's spirit was creating— was bringing form and solidarity and significance out of the chaos. The message of the Bible, from cover to cover, is that God's spirit is still "moving upon the face of the waters." The self-same spirit present at Creation is still active. And God's spirit still seeks to bring order and harmony and beauty out of the chaos of our lives.

One night on a dark, storm-tossed sea, the disciples of Jesus huddled in fear in a boat that was being thrown about by monstrous waves. The ocean had become a horrible force that threatened their very lives. Suddenly, Jesus appeared; walking across the waves, he came to them in the midst of their fright and brought order, peace, and tranquility out of their chaos.

Perhaps the most astounding of all of the accounts of God's bringing order out of chaos—and the one that is almost too good to be true—is the story on which we focus on this third Sunday of Lent—the account of the Resurrection and appearance of Jesus. The Crucifixion and the subsequent events brought confusion and dismay to the lives of those who loved and followed Jesus. Yet, the women spread the word—the unbelievable word—"He is not dead. He is risen!" God created—even in the chaos of his own Son's death.

It is too good to be true. So we rub our eyes and look again to see if what is before us is really there. Can it be true that God is really at work among us? Can it be that the Good News is really true? The message of the gospel for us today and always is that God is at work among us. The faith that we claim demands that we have a perspective different from that which we receive from the six o'clock news.

We ask the question, "Does the universe have meaning?" The Bible is certain that it does. The Creation account promises that it does. Creation is not a finished story. It happens anew each moment for those who have the faith to perceive it. In God, all things belong to the same consistent pattern. The universe—and our lives—are meant to fit together and to have meaning. If we can trust that life began in goodness, we can go forward into life with courage and gallant expectation. The faith that is expressed in the first two verses of Genesis is not different from the faith that can come to any and every honest seeker.

Over whatever is waste and void and confusion, God's spirit moves—moves deliberately and creatively according to a holy purpose that nothing can be strong enough to turn aside. This is good to remember when life seems empty or overpowering or when darkness seems to descend upon us. The spirit of God has not vanished from our universe. God's spirit is here among us—in the midst of our own personal and painfully private chaos.

Pain, turmoil, and even chaos are often part of the reality of our lives—on both the cosmic and personal levels. There will be times when watching the six o'clock news is a painfully depressing activity. There will be days and even weeks in our own lives when God seems far away or even absent. There will be days when nothing goes right, when crises follow one after the other, when there seems to be little reason to go on. These are days like those the disciples experienced after the Crucifixion dashed all their hopes and dreams and aspirations.

These are the days when we need to remember the power of God to create. It is in these times that we need to give ourselves more fully to God and to trust God in spite of the dilemma in which we find ourselves. It is in these times that we need to cling to our faith—to believe—even when it is too good to be true.

This sermon was preached in April 1988 in Charlotte, North Carolina, at St. John's Baptist Church.

Blessed Be She

Luke 11:27-28

Cindy Harp Johnson

One day Adam and Seth were plowing the field, watering a dusty furrow by the sweat of their brows. When they stopped to rest, Seth's gaze wandered to the horizon, where he saw a lush, verdant garden.

"Dad! Dad! What's that?" he asked.

"Well, son, it's a sad story," Adam replied. "That's where we used to live. But then your mother ate us out of house and home."

And the world has been a hard place from which to wring a blessing for a woman ever since! Since then, every choice we make regarding our lives is suspect. We choose to remain single and are subject to the speculation that there's something fundamentally wrong with us. You know, like a hairy back, a stone for a heart, or napalm breath in the morning—some hidden affliction that keeps us from being wanted by anybody. We choose to marry, and walk the aisle amidst the sighs of relief from those who believed that we couldn't have made it on our own.

We choose not to have children, and we're accused of idolatrous self-interest. We choose to bear children, and we bear the nagging notion of having wasted our market-place potential. We choose careers outside the home and confront the verdict that the woman for hire is the downfall of the family. We choose careers that heretofore have been chosen only by men, and Katie bar the door! That's when the name-calling really begins!

There seems no option for a woman today that doesn't fall under suspicion; that in itself could prompt us to believe that the options themselves are the problem. Whatever happened to the good old days when everyone's roles were defined? when people knew their cues, their lines, their assigned places? when it was easy to bless a job well done because there were standard job descriptions?

Like in Jesus' day! Things were so much simpler then. Men took care of the world. Women took care of the home and had babies. When a man took care of his affairs in such a way that he was able to provide himself a home, he was applauded. When a woman took care of the home provided her by her husband and had babies, she was applauded. Everyone knew the value of his or her work, and everyone derived his or her value from it.

The woman who pronounced the blessing in our Scripture lesson knew the value of the work of a mother. She knew Mary had done well to produce such a son as Jesus. And she knew such a mother was worthy of praise: "Blessed be she who bore you from her womb, who gave you the nourishment of her breasts! Blessed be she who fulfilled the reason for her existence!" (author's paraphrase).

What has happened to such clarity of purpose for women? Where did we lose it?

Let there be no mistake about it. We lost it in the teachings of Jesus, who redefined our understanding of the yardstick for blessedness. Blessed be not those who fulfill arbitrary roles imposed on them for simplicity or convenience, but blessed be those who choose to fulfill the will of God.

So the question now becomes, "What is the will of God for women?" And to find the answer, we must start at the very beginning.

Look with me, if you will, at the first account of Creation, where we have the record of God's original intention for women. I want us to read this passage literally this morning, allowing it to speak for itself. But to do that, we need a little Hebrew lesson, for something is lost in the translation from the original language into English, indicated by the awkward grammar in Genesis 1:26-28.

Look at verse 26. Have you ever wondered why the first phrase says, "Let us make man (singular) in our image, after our likeness," but then the next phrase says, "and let them (plural) have dominion"? And then in the next verse, "So God created man in his own image, in the image of God he created him," then the pronouns jump again to the plural, "Male and female he created them" (RSV).

The terrible English is the result of the mistranslation of the Hebrew word *adam*, which literally means "people," not "male of the species" or "man." Of the 510 times *adam* is used in the Old Testament, it can rarely be proven conclusively that it indicates "a man."[1] And so if we insert "people" wherever *adam* is found in the text, or wherever a pronoun referring to *adam* is found, our translation, the grammar, and our understanding of God's intention for women are corrected. Listen to what this passage, read properly, really says:

> *Then God said, "Let us make people in our image, after our likeness; and let people have dominion over the fish of the sea, and over the birds of the air, and over the cattle, and over all the earth, and over every creeping thing that creeps upon the earth." So God created people in his own image, in the image of God he created people; male and female he created people. And God blessed people, and God said to people, "Be fruitful and multiply, and fill the earth and subdue it; and have dominion over the fish of the sea and over the birds of the air and over every living thing that moves upon the earth."*
>
> *(author's translation based on the RSV)*

This, then, is God's will and intention for women as manifested in creation. And its expression is found through three avenues. First of all, women were created in the image of God, to mirror *a reflection of God.* In the character of women was planted a seed of the likeness of God, including rationality, moral choice, responsible action, and self-transcendence.[2] The likeness of God also implies a capacity for *a relationship with God,* through which women are enabled to act out God-behaviors in the world. This is the second expression of God's will for women: that they be God's agents within creation, that they continue the creative processes, that they fill the earth, subdue it, and have dominion. And just as the image of God could not be contained in one kind of person, requiring by necessity both sexes, and because the work of God cannot be completed by one kind of person, the third intention of God for women is to perform their task *in partnership with men.* God blessed both of them, male and female, giving both of them, male and female, the same tasks in the world.

The idea of partnership is also reflected in the second creation account. The order of events in this version is different because it's a different interpretation of how the world began, but the partnership theme is common to both of the narratives. Look at Genesis 2:18 for another expression of God's intention for women. And as before, let's read this passage literally, which means, guess what? We need another Hebrew lesson.

The Lord says here, "It is not good that man should be alone; I will make him an *ezer*" (RSV). Now the problem with *ezer* is not so much that we don't translate it literally but that the literal English translation of *ezer* has become attached to a connotation that is foreign to the Hebrew concept.

I'll show you what I mean. This same word is found in Psalm 121:1-2 (NRSV). Some of us may know this from memory: "I will lift up my eyes to the hills. From whence does my *ezer* come? My *ezer* comes from the LORD, who made heaven and earth." It's also found in Psalm 146:3,5 (NRSV): "Put not you trust in princes, in a son of man, in whom there is no *ezer*. . . . Happy is he whose *ezer* is the God of Jacob, whose hope is in the LORD . . ." And Psalm 33:20 (NRSV): "Our soul waits for the LORD; he is our *ezer* and shield."

This Hebrew word is used twenty-one times in the Old Testament. Sixteen times it refers to the aid of a superior force that alters a situation for the betterment of those involved.[3] Five times it refers to the cooperating efforts of human partners, the sum total of whose efforts produce a greater effect than their individual efforts could have. In no case does *ezer* refer to secondary assistance for a primary task—unless we make Genesis 2:18 the one exception.[4] And that's what we do when we translate *ezer* as "helper" or "helpmeet" here. If we could read, "It's not good that man should be alone; I will make a helper fit for him," without instantly thinking that Adam needed someone to wash out his socks, "helper" could be an accurate translation. But since our perception of the meaning of this text has been supplied by historical tradition rather than sound principles of biblical interpretation, we cannot read "helper" in this passage and understand it as the Hebrew intended.

We must instead use another word, as the *New English Bible* dared to do by translating *ezer* as "partner." This passage then becomes, "It is not good for man to be alone. I will provide him a partner." The chronology of woman's creation may be different in the two Genesis accounts, but God's intention for woman remains consistent: She is a full-fledged partner for bringing to fruition God's purposes in the world.

So now we have established that women and men are created side by side in creation, made for the purpose of mutuality and unity. But what about their roles? Don't they have different roles to play?

Indeed they do. Remember, that was one of the purposes for God creating female and male in the first place: that there might be different kinds of people to perform the different kinds of tasks in the world. So am I saying that there are scripts we're supposed to be following? that there are cues, lines, and assigned places to return us to the good old days of standard job descriptions?

Well, no, not exactly—which brings us back to Jesus and his redefinition of our yardstick for blessedness. Blessed be not those who fulfill arbitrary roles imposed on them for simplicity or convenience. But blessed be those who choose to fulfill the will of God.

And Jesus was a person who knew something about this role-versus-the-will-of-God dilemma. At every turn someone was telling him who and what he should be. Even in the verses preceding our Lukan lesson, he is arguing about his identity. People piped, expecting him to dance. People played a dirge, expecting him to mourn. They provided the soldiers, expecting him to march. They provided the swords, expecting him to war. But at every turn came the same reply: "I have come to do only the will of God."

And it was a disruptive message indeed to imply that the neatly ordered categories of life no longer applied if they didn't comply with the will of God. Everybody knew that tax collectors and sinners were to be despised, but Jesus treated them as valuable people. Everybody knew that Pharisees and scribes were to be honored above all, but Jesus reminded them of their fallibility. People were expected to marry, but Jesus taught them there is also the choice of being a eunuch for God. Children were to be seen and not heard, but Jesus paid them special attention. Women were property whose place was in the home, but Jesus related to them as human beings, encouraging them to learn and have a part in his ministry even outside their homes. Jesus constantly encouraged each individual to seek God's individual direction for his or her life and refuted any other claim of authority.

And so we do have specific roles for our lives, but they are not assigned places with standard job descriptions determined by gender or tradition or any artificial limitation. They are defined by our capacity to reflect the image of God, and our willingness to perform God's work in the world in partnership with all other people.

How then can a woman wring a blessing from this world? By refusing to conform to any mold except that provided by God. How then can we bless women? By according them all the roles God intends, and by applauding the fulfillment of their God-assigned tasks.

There's a prayer I pray to myself right before I preach. If I'm particularly nervous about a speaking assignment, or if my preparation hasn't gone as well as I would have liked it to, the prayer slips out as, "Father, forgive me, for I know not what I do!" And yet when I am at ease, and am confident about the word from the Lord which I'm about to deliver, my prayer goes like this: "Accept this service that I do; I do it unto Thee."

And I always wondered where that line came from, how it was submerged in my subconscious, ready to spring forward before any ministry task. But on one vacation at my parent's home, I discovered its source. Hanging there near my mother's sink, where I had stood countless times doing dishes, was "The Kitchen Prayer." It's a poem by Klara Munkres that begins with, "Lord of all pots and pans and things, since I've not time to be / a saint by doing lovely things or watching late with Thee," and ends with the words, "Accept this service that I do, I do it unto Thee."

And so it was there, performing one choice of a role for a woman, that I began to learn that the Lord of all pots and pans and things lays a vast array of choices before me—and that whenever I choose a task to which the Lord has directed me, doing it to fulfill God's will for my life, it is an acceptable service, and I am a blessed woman.

We have come here today to worship as we honor mothers. And yet we want to do it right; we want to do it well. So we do not praise motherhood at the expense of the other avenues available to women. To do so would be to invalidate the legitimacy of the many roles God calls women to play. To do so would be to resign mothers to a one-dimensional existence.

Neither do we honor mothers as marionettes who are mindlessly following a script. We come to uphold you as whole beings who have responded to God's will for your life. We come to marvel at the timelessness of the part you play in the world as we know it. We come to acknowledge the godly courage and sacrifice your task has required. And we come to say as Jesus did, "Blessed be she who hears the word of God and keeps it!"

In a conversation Jesus had with a woman named Martha, he told her that only one thing was needful. Go, now, in search of that one thing God has in store for your life, that in the accomplishing of it, you might be blessed. Amen!

This sermon was preached as a Mother's Day sermon in May 1988, at Fourth Baptist Church, Upperco, Maryland.

NOTES

1. Ralph Elliott, *The Message of Genesis* (Nashville: Broadman Press, 1961), 39, as cited by Ludwig Kohler, *Old Testament Theology*, trans. A.S. Todd (Philadelphia: Westminster Press, 1953), 88.

2. These ideas reflect the writings of Minette Drumwright, from the study guide *Women in the Church* (Nashville: Seminary Extension Department of the Seminaries of the Southern Baptist Convention, 1988), 19-26.

3. Drumwright, 21.

4. Russel C. Prohl, *Woman in the Church* (Grand Rapids: Wm. B. Eerdmans Publishing Co., 1957), 34.

Going Home
by a Different Way

Matthew 2:1-12

Elizabeth Smith Bellinger

I sat beside the bed of an eighty-seven-year-old black woman as she lay dying. My back ached from holding her hand, and fatigue had settled upon my shoulders.

She had verbally wandered all afternoon from place to place, from person to person and back again. Her journey toward death seemed endless. She seemed lost and desolate. I confess to you that my mind had shifted into neutral, and I had stopped listening to her wanderings.

And then as so often happens when we stop the "laying on of ears," her words slapped me to attention. She looked at me directly, with recognition, and said, "Reverend Libby, I'm going home, I'm going home!" I echoed her words and she said again, "I'm going home. I'm going home a different way, but I'm going home."

She drifted off again on her move toward death and shortly thereafter went home to be with her Lord. Her words haunted me. "I'm going home a different way." Was she mentally going to the home of her childhood, or the home of her years as a bride and young mother? Was she returning to the home she left before entering the nursing center? Or was the way to heaven different than she imagined, than we all imagine, and was she sharing that insight with me? Going home, but home by a different way.

Home. We all have images of home, most of them positive. Home is where they want you. You can more or less assume that you'll be welcomed in the end. Home is a source of security.

However, home is not so much a place of residence as it is a quality of relationship. For the last eleven years, the Southern Baptist Convention has seemed less and less like home to us. Convention faces are not familiar anymore—and certainly not welcoming. Suspicious stares are met with suspicious stares; words are guarded and conversations contrived. We feel like unwelcome guests in our own home. Our sense of belonging is gone; our relationships have changed; our sense of security is missing.

The feeling of insecurity and discomfort extends beyond the annual gathering and radiates throughout the states and regions, to the mission fields home and abroad, to the institutions and agencies. Us versus them. Where is the sense of family we once had with each other? What is the deadly cancer that spreads in our midst?

I read a passage of Scripture this evening that is quite familiar to you all. The Magi, some oriental wise guys who traveled guided by a star toward their destination, needed aid, so they stopped to seek counsel from the local king. Herod was the authority in the area. He had been empowered by the Romans and the Jews. He'd be able to give them direction to the one they sought and then send them back upon their journey home. But the passage tells us that, warned in a dream of Herod's scheme, they went home by a different way. Here in these familiar words in Luke, I heard echoed the words of a dying woman and wondered at their meaning.

Herod offered nothing but death—to the Magi possibly, to the infant King certainly. Herod was a person infused with power and yet with such insecurity that any threat had to be dealt with swiftly and completely, whether family or friend or foe. Threatened by the birth of a possible king, he had to have his informants. He was troubled, and when Herod was troubled, all of Jerusalem lived hard. He had to gather together all his henchmen for a private meeting in Atlanta so they'd have the same story to tell the local press when they asked, "What is this star? What does it mean?" So they consulted the original manuscripts and pointed these eastern kings toward Bethlehem. He dispatched them to this town as spies and filled their minds with half-truths in order to secure control. Herod promised to worship, but hatred ruled his heart.

The Magi, warned in a dream of Herod's scheme, went home by a different way. They took away Herod's power, listened to their visions, and sought a safe way to return home. You can picture them, servants in tow, loading up their camels and saying, "Let's get home another way." They knew Herod was not who he said he was. Their perceptions were changed. The evil was seen through the revelation given them, and they were released from their obligation to honor the king and went home.

It isn't always easy to go home, especially if obstacles block the trail. The Magi would have had to take a very circuitous route in order not to be discovered by Herod's henchmen. It probably would have increased the length of their journey considerably, but safety and familiarity would welcome them when they completed the pilgrimage.

The Magi had originally given power to Herod. They needed information from him; they needed direction. They found what they sought. But then, warned in a dream of Herod's scheme, they went home by another way.

While I was thinking of their need to get home, the image of Dorothy in *The Wizard of Oz* came to mind. You remember Dorothy and Toto? She missed the safety and comfort of home. All that was familiar, all those who loved her were there in Kansas. She had to get home. But how was she going to do it? How was she to find the way?

By the Great and Powerful, Wonderful Wizard of Oz! Now those of us who have relished the viewing of this movie year after year know that the Wizard wasn't a wizard. He was not great and powerful. He was just a man, another Kansan who had lost his way. His power, his might, came from Dorothy's perception of who he was. She reacted to his special effects, to all his smoke and flames and amplified voice. The press agent of Oz, good witch Glenda, had told Dorothy about him. The citizens of Oz confirmed her press release, and Dorothy gave power to the Wizard so he could show her how to go home. Now fortunately for Dorothy, this wizard was a good wizard, and so he did her no harm and actually helped her friends claim their own power. But unfortunately, this is not the case in real life.

Did you know we have wizards in our midst? There is the wizard of Houston, the wizard of Dallas, the wizard of Memphis, the wizard of Atlanta. We give power to these wizards. We have our wizards here in Southern Baptist Oz. But one of the problems is that they are not good wizards, not wizards of blessing and empowerment. They have taken the color picture and painted it black and white. The landscape no longer looks familiar or inviting. Contrasts are dark and bleak. Our security is gone because all our relationships are called into question. Home has disappeared from the picture. Like the Magi and Dorothy, we give wizards their power. It is our perception of who they are that gives them power. We believe the press releases we read. We believe the tapes we hear that spread the news of their universal plan for good. In the book entitled *The Neverending Story*, by Michael Ende, the kingdom in this story is being attacked. It is being eaten up, devoured by Nothingness. That is the way I see the Southern Baptist Convention; it is being swallowed up in chunks by ugly, dark nothingness. Huge holes have appeared in what once was good, and it is frightening.

Now let me be honest with you: the convention was good before, but not perfect. There are parts I would like to see swallowed up, but the growing nothingness that is slowly inching its way across is like a cancer slowly spreading out its ugly fingers. It is up to each one of us to be engaged in the search for its cure.

So what can we do? you ask yourselves. As a beginning, we can affirm our traditions, our historical roots, so to speak. Now let me emphasize when we link home, when we link security, to an institution, our foundations are shaky. Whatever real security we find in this convention stems from God's presence. However, make no mistake about it, God's presence can be experienced in other conventions and other denominations.

Biblically speaking, secure persons have found tradition as a source of strength. Now, I'm well aware that tradition can be a crippling burden. However, I also know that tradition can be an enabling incentive for us to deal with the Herods in our midst. We need to affirm the priesthood of the believer, the autonomy of the local church, the need for servant leadership, the significance of adult believer's baptism. People without tradition are deprived of a sense of continuity with the past, an identity for the present, and the ability to cope with the future. Now that doesn't mean we don't change and grow while hearing the leading of the Spirit, but it does suggest that some realities endure. It is from these historical traditions that we get our strength and sense of home.

What I have just described has been a model for group response. But what about individually? Let me raise some possibilities. Avoid kingly audiences and big to-dos. Our call as ministers is to proclaim release to the captives, the oppressed, and the downtrodden—not to hold church services during Superbowl Sunday. Christ's life was one of simplicity, poverty, and charity—and that is our model. Remember with whom you are dealing. A king who would slaughter the innocents will not cut a deal for you. Ask yourselves, "What games am I playing in order to get that First Baptist Church pastorate or to keep my job at this institution?" Where is your integrity? You are dealing with people who will comb your camel's fur until they find the trace amounts of your frankincense, gold, and myrrh. They will comb the books, pamphlets, monographs, speeches, prayers, sermons to find whatever they seek.

Now it is a miracle that I'm here tonight to preach this word to you. I should be silent, if some people could have their way. But the age of change is blowing through our convention, a spirit that I hope will change us into more Christlike people of faith. It is a spirit of change that is going to require us to go home by a different way.

But remember, Herod's always out there, and he's probably already got your card on file. The wizards know how to get you to give them power. It's a cinch; if you give an inch, they are going to take a mile.

We are a pilgrim people. We have gotten this far guided by the star. The winds of change are blowing, and we must seek counsel from above. In a crunch, when the pressure is on and you must act courageously, or on an ordinary day, when in normal ways you simply must act honestly, remember that tradition—especially salvation history—is our source of strength, and that faith in Jesus Christ will guide us home by a different way!

This sermon was preached in June 1988 in San Antonio, Texas, at the Southern Baptist Forum.

A Wedding Sermon

Jan Fuller Carruthers

My friends,
there is a small and shameful secret that I want to tell you.
It's not a secret at all.
You know it already, of course.
But it's a secret because we do not speak of it with each other.
Each one holds it close in our darkest corners,
thinking of it as poison.

It is a small secret,
small as a sigh in the long night,
but it is a powerful builder.
It builds great walls and deep moats
and sharpens swords of wit and wisdom.
Because it is a secret, we cannot let each other know it.
But because we all know it,
we are all conspirators in this silence.

Here is the secret:
I don't believe anyone could ever understand me.
Worse yet, if anyone did understand me,
surely they wouldn't accept me, let alone love me.
I am alone.

Adolescents are graced with sufficient misery to say it: Nobody loves me. Nobody understands me. But that's why we don't like adolescents. They know too much, and they can't shut up about it. It is embarrassing. And so we go along, in silence, thinking we are fooling each other, building walls that are sufficiently stout to prevent anyone

from knowing the truth. That is our shame. Worse, we know we are
fooling ourselves, and that is our terror. And so we are amazed and astonished at Denise and Patrick today.
We are delighted and filled with joy. For today they have broken the
code; they have stepped outside our conspiracy, which keeps us locked
in loneliness and terror. They have spoken the truth to each other in
love. Patrick has said to Denise, I know the secret fear you bear within
you, for it is my fear too. It is my secret as well. But I love you, knowing
this. No need, my dear, for walls and wedges and labyrinthine ploys.
I accept you.

And Denise has said to Patrick, I have known for some time that
we have shared the secret and in sharing it have deprived it of shame.
For you have thrown a bridge across the moat and invited me to enter,
and I have walked and wandered in your open heart. I have swung
wide the door that sealed my spiritual chambers, and I have grown to
love the sound of your sure step within my mind.

This is the good news that I announce to you today. The witness
of Patrick and Denise testifies to all of us a word from God. So
convinced have they become that they now commit, in absurd intimacy and trust, to the point that they can fling their freedom into
fidelity—so convinced are they that the One who first established
them in life has also given them this life together.

The Greek language uses the same word for secret and mystery.
This is the word used by Paul when he speaks of marriage. It is, he
says, a great mystery and refers to a greater One—the way God is with
us. Paul says, look and see what a miracle it is when a man and woman
leap beyond their limits and join in this most fragile and stunning of
loves. If this astonishes you, as it should, learn from it how God is
with all God's children, all the time.

In their union this day, God says to us, I know your secret hearts,
and I will never give up on you. No matter how unfaithful you might
be, I forgive and forget the breaking of promises and hurts inflicted
by you, I seek to give you whatever you need and never what you
deserve. I accept you as you are, even when you are being most
unlovable. I will never leave you or give up on you but will seek after
you, and I willingly assume the pain of your estranged actions to the

end that we might be reconciled and made one.

Patrick and Denise have known each other, and have accepted the small, sad secret, and laughed. They have made covenant. God has known us all along, that we fear being known, that we fear being alone, and even more that we fear being accepted as such limited, wretched beings.

And in the flesh of our Lord Jesus, God has laughed, and said, that's all right. Let me do the leaping. Unless those who commit themselves to each other in marriage dwell in Christ's love, they can never be faithful to their promise to stay together when they break their promises to have, hold, and cherish each other. It is Christ's love that holds us when we look across the bed covers or the kitchen table and notice a stranger in that one we love. In good days and in bad, promise to love each other with the love measured by the kind of love God has for each of us.

Denise and Patrick, be a sign for us. Teach us of faithful love, of fidelity, of truth-telling in love, and of the mystery of intimate aloneness. Be a sign of God's grace for all the world.

And we will be signs for you. We rejoice at this victory won by the fine flash of your freedom to be faithful to each other. And we support you, promise to pray for you in good days and in bad, for the web of trust is fragile and the doing and living of truth in this world is a gesture never to be assumed. You are a sign of reconciliation and peace in our midst; we will be for you a sign of support and trust.

Secrets turn to mysteries in the dark places of God's freedom. Faced with wonder, we grow fearful. Established with freedom, we are charmed.

Blessed be the Lord, who works in strange and wonderful ways among the sons and daughters of our earth.

Amen.

This sermon was preached in June 1988 in Roanoke, Virginia, at a wedding performed in the Hollins College Chapel.

Upside-down Blessing

Psalm 128; Mark 10:2-16

Jann Aldredge-Clanton

The popular song by Ray Stevens entitled "Jesus Wear a Rolex?" makes fun of those preachers who believe that they deserve all the riches of this world and the next. They wear Rolex watches, drive expensive cars, and live in luxurious houses. They preach a wealth, health, success gospel— if you become a Christian, then God will shower material blessings upon you. If you do God's will, you'll have something to show for it. This materialistic gospel is widespread. You can even buy Christian designer jeans with the sign of the fish and the name "Jesus" stenciled in golden thread on the hip pocket. Advertising these jeans is a sign that reads, "Witness with Style."

Down through history people have believed that tangible blessings are signs of God's favor. Such is the theology of the writer of Psalm 128. According to this psalm, Jesus did not reverence God and walk in God's ways because those who do have certain rewards. And Jesus did not have these rewards. Jesus did not get to enjoy the material rewards of labor. Jesus had no wife and children. Jesus did not see the prosperity of Jerusalem. Jesus did not have long life. Traditional Hebrew wisdom literature would not call Jesus' life blessed.

Rabbi Harold Kushner struggles with this Hebrew concept of blessing upon those who reverence God. After his fourteen-year-old son Aaron died of a disease that causes rapid aging, Kushner wrote a book called *Why Bad Things Happen to Good People*. Kushner, who had spent his life reverencing God and teaching others about God, could not understand why his son died. Kushner laments, "I felt a deep, aching sense of unfairness. I had been a good person. I had tried to do what was right in the sight of God. I was living a more religiously committed life than most people. I knew people not so religious who had large, healthy families. I believed that I was following God's ways and doing God's work. How could this be happening to my family?"

Jesus came bringing a new covenant and a new concept of blessing. He turns the Hebrew concept of blessing upside down. Jesus Christ teaches and demonstrates that blessing comes through suffering, not prosperity. Christ said, "Blessed are those who mourn . . . blessed are those who are persecuted for righteousness' sake" (Matthew 5:4,10, RSV). Christ was "crowned with glory and honor because of the suffering of death" (Hebrews 2:9, RSV). Christ calls us to follow this pathway to blessing through suffering (Matthew 16:24).

Now this does not mean that we should go out seeking suffering or self-inflicted pain, like some who think they obtain virtue or blessing by walking on hot coals. Suffering comes to each one of us uninvited. Blessing for the Christian comes through accepting God's comfort and strength in the midst of this suffering that is part of our human condition. Blessing comes to us also by following Christ in suffering for righteousness' sake.

Corrie and Bessie ten Boom suffered all kinds of indignities and tortures in concentration camps because they tried to hide Jews from the Nazis. They suffered because they did what was right. In protecting Jews from the atrocities of Hitler, they did what Christ would do. They suffered for righteousness' sake and received God's blessing. Bessie especially felt blessing in the midst of her suffering. She felt enough strength from God to enable her to forgive even the cruel guards in the concentration camps.

Blessing comes from having convictions and standing by them, no matter what. Sandra held the position of personnel director of a large, prestigious company. This position was the fulfillment of her vocational dreams. She had worked hard to get to this point in her career. Not long after she became personnel director, she began to get pressure from one of the vice-presidents of the company to put the applications of African Americans and Hispanics on the bottom of the pile. Sandra felt that this blatant racial discrimination went against her Christian principles. When she refused to discriminate, she lost her job. Following Christ often means suffering for righteousness' sake. But Christ promises that those who suffer for doing right will be blessed. The blessing comes through suffering, not through success and prosperity.

Preacher and author Tony Campolo says that the church is losing
a generation of youth not because we've made the gospel too hard but
because we've made it too easy. Young people want a challenge; they
don't want to grow up and just become "yuppies." They want a cause
worth giving their lives to. In the church we do youth a disservice by
expecting too little of them. In the short run we may gain a large youth
group by catering to their every wish, with endless fun and games, but
we'll lose them when they discover a lack of challenge and depth and
meaning.

Christ shows us that blessing comes through blessing others. Christ
teaches us to bless those least likely to receive blessing: "Love your
enemies, and pray for those who persecute you" (Matthew 5:44,
RSV). Myron Madden, in a book called *The Power to Bless,* says that
Christians have the high privilege to bless in the name of God. He
says that too many children have grown up without the blessing of
their parents. But the power of blessing is stronger than the power of
curse. In Christ's strength we can bless those who curse us and thus
take away the power of the curse. In the name of Christ we can bless
those who have been cursed by others and thus take away the power
of the curse.

The society of Jesus' day put little value on children. The disciples
thought Jesus was too important to waste time with children. "And
they were bringing children to him, that he might touch them; and
the disciples rebuked them" (Mark 10:13, RSV). But Jesus offers the
children one of the most beautiful and complete blessings recorded in
Scripture: "Let the children come to me, do not hinder them; for to
such belongs the kingdom of God. Truly, I say to you, whoever does
not receive the kingdom of God like a child shall not enter it" (Mark
10:14-15, RSV). And then Mark tells us that Jesus "took them in his
arms and blessed them, laying his hands upon them" (Mark 10:16,
RSV).

Following Jesus means loving the least, the weakest, the most
devalued, the most neglected. LaTasha lay crying in her hospital crib.
It was not the strong, demanding cry of a newborn baby, but faint
sobs with gasps in between. LaTasha's cry had the pitiful, resigned tone
of one whose cries went unheard and unanswered. The nurses tried
to give her as much attention as they could, but with so many other

children to care for, they could not stay with LaTasha very long. There was never a mother, father, grandparent, uncle, or aunt in the room with this three-month-old baby. LaTasha's parents, unmarried teenagers and IV drug users, abandoned LaTasha. An apartment manager had found this emaciated infant, just barely alive, in the apartment where the couple stayed for a little while and then left without notice. A social worker finally tracked down the parents, but they were unfit and unwilling to care for LaTasha. A series of tests at the hospital led to the diagnosis of AIDS. This dreadful disease was all her parents had given her. After several months, the social worker had not been able to place LaTasha in an adoptive or a foster home. To place a black baby with such a background and with AIDS seemed impossible. A little while later, a woman appeared at the hospital, saying that she had started procedures to adopt LaTasha. She said that she had heard about LaTasha from a friend and decided to take her. Incredulous nurses and doctors asked her why she wanted this little girl. She replied, "She needs someone to love her and take care of her. She's a child of God too."

All of us find it easy to love those who love us, to love the loveable, the respectable, the beautiful. We can easily love those who can give us something in return. It's harder to care for somebody who can't or won't give anything to us—a helpless child or elderly person or poverty-stricken person who has nothing to give and may not even give us a thank you. Jesus said that if we love only those who love us, we won't receive spiritual rewards. Christ's blessing comes from giving blessing even to the despised and the least of our sisters and brothers. Blessing brings life both to the one giving and the one receiving the blessing.

Christ's blessing restores God's ideal. In Mark 10:2-9, Christ distinguishes between traditional law and God's ideal. Not all institutions and laws recorded in Scripture express the divine ideal. God does not authorize everything God tolerates. God's ideal for marriage from the beginning of creation is a permanent, mutual relationship. But according to Mosaic law in the Old Testament, a man could divorce his wife if he wrote her a bill of divorce stating his reasons for wanting the divorce (Deuteronomy 24:1-4). The woman, however, could not divorce her husband. Jesus said that this law does not express God's original intent. Moses gave this law because of "your hardness of heart"—in other words, because of human sinfulness. This law of Moses was an improvement over pagan society, which allowed men to divorce their wives for no reason and with no written statement. But Jesus came with a new covenant and a new blessing. His blessings turned the traditional Jewish law upside down to restore God's ideal for male and female. Christ points us back to God's good creation in which male and female are created equally in God's image and are thus capable of sustaining a mutual covenant relationship for a lifetime. Christ's blessing comes as we restore the divine ideal in all our relationships.

At times we all would settle for the more tangible blessings promised in Hebrew wisdom literature. Maybe we're not tempted by Rolex watches, Mercedes Benz cars, or swimming pools. We may realize how superficial and temporal these things are. But we would all like the tangible blessings of something to show for our labor, such as healthy and happy families, and long life.

Jesus comes to us today offering far more profound blessings, those blessings that satisfy the deep-down, eternal longings of our hearts. Christ's kind of blessing may seem upside down to us because a cross comes with Christ's kind of blessing—a strange kind of blessing. The blessing Christ has to give comes not from seeking the blessing for ourselves but from giving it away to others. Christ's blessing comes not from maintaining the status quo but from turning the status quo upside down to restore God's ideal.

Are we willing to take up our cross and follow Christ? Are we willing to go against the flow, to be change agents working toward God's ideal? Are we willing to love the neglected and rejected, the last and the least? If we are, we will hear Christ say to us, "Come, O blessed of God [my Father], inherit the kingdom prepared for you from the foundation of the world" (Matthew 25:34, RSV). The kingdom of abundant life. The kingdom of eternal life. Only this everlasting blessing of Christ can satisfy the deepest longings of our souls.

This sermon was preached in August 1988 in Waco, Texas, at St. John's United Methodist Church.

Keepers of the Fire

Leviticus 6:8-13; 1 Thessalonians 5:1-24

Anne Thomas Neil

An article in the *Christian Century* entitled "The Business of the Church"[1] was memorable for me because it affirmed many of my own concerns during the decade of the eighties, concerns about the lack of true vitality in many of our churches. In 1980, while my husband, Lloyd, and I were still in Ghana, West Africa, it became necessary for me to return to the States. During the four weeks I was here, I worshiped in three different churches and talked with family and friends regarding the life and ministry of their respective churches. Upon my return to Ghana, I said to Lloyd, "I grieve for the church in America."

Why would I make such a statement? Because both in worship and conversation I experienced a kind of heaviness of spirit with a minimum of joy and expectancy—a kind of malaise or lethargy. In Ghana, everyone had experienced "the bottoming out of the economy." Food was scarce and hard to come by; available medical care was deteriorating rapidly; the government was unstable and unpredictable. In three years we had experienced three different governments and two major currency devaluations. It was common to put your car in a petrol line for a two- to three-day wait, hoping that when the tanker came you might be able to buy ten gallons of fuel. The university students with whom I was working literally prayed for soap and toothpaste. The schools at all levels were trying to keep their doors open in a hand-to-mouth economy. Humanly speaking, the situation was grim.

But in the midst of these deplorable social and economic circumstances, the church across the street from us was alive, exciting, and growing. To get a seat in the large sanctuary, you needed to be there at least thirty minutes before the worship service began. Sunday school

classes were everywhere—in the educational building, under trees, on
the porch of the pastorium. By the time the worship service began,
the congregation had usually spilled over to the outside and worshipers
surrounded the sanctuary. It was energizing just to watch people as they walked briskly toward
the church in a spirit of expectancy. They were embodying Paul's
directives to the church at Thessalonica:

Be joyful always;
Pray continually;
Give thanks in all circumstances, . . .
Do not put out the Spirit's fire.
—1 Thessalonians 5:16-19, NIV

On Monday morning these same worshipers were at work in the
marketplace, in offices, in classrooms, in hospitals and clinics, on
farms, in their taxis. There they were bearing their convincing witness
to the transforming and radical message of Jesus Christ—the Good
News of the gospel. Joyfully, prayerfully, thankfully, and expectantly,
the Spirit's fire burned brightly in their lives. It was no wonder that
Sunday after Sunday others came forward to confess faith in Christ
and to request membership in the church, the community of faith.
This church was no isolated case. Much was happening, and continues
to happen, in the churches in Ghana and all across sub-Saharan Africa.

In contrast, the opening sentence in the *Christian Century* article
is a remark by Wood's philosopher colleague, "Nothing is happening."
Initially, Wood was not sure just what his friend was addressing. He
soon found out his friend was lamenting the lack of vitality in most
of the well-established Protestant and Catholic churches in America.

Wood suggests, "This would seem a howling misconception." Our
churches are bustling places busily pursuing our many worthwhile
activities—peace-and-justice seminars, inclusive-language work-
shops, spirituality seminars for developing the inner life, meals-on-
wheels, hunger and housing concerns, support groups to sustain the
sick and grieving, and on and on. Wood asks, "Are not these salutary
endeavors signs of church vitality? Why the protest that nothing is
going on?" The philosopher friend meant that as worthy as these
activities are, none is distinctively Christian. He contends that a busy

and active church may thus be sick unto death while giving the appearance of vibrant health.

Could it be that in our affluent society the church has taught and encouraged us to do good without instructing us in the Christian conviction that real goodness is rooted in the holiness of God? Do we minister out of a sense of moral "oughtness" rather than from the holy fire within?

Probing further, Wood quotes from a recent book by John Leith, the distinguished Presbyterian theologian and doctrinal historian. The book, *The Reformed Imperative,* carries the subtitle *What the Church Has to Say That No One Else Can Say.* I quote:

> "*The primary source of the malaise of the church is the loss of a distinctive Christian message and of the theological and biblical competence that made its preaching effective. Sermons fail to mediate the presence and grace of God. . . . The only skill the preacher has—or the church, for that matter—which is not found with greater excellence somewhere else, is theology, in particular the skill to interpret and apply the Word of God in sermon, teaching, and pastoral care. This is the great service which the minister and the church can render the world. Why should anyone come to church for what can be better found somewhere else?*"[2]

I affirm that Christian faith stands solely on its unique message of divine redemption through Jesus Christ. This is the Easter story. Wood contends that this emphasis is not to divorce the church's proclamation from its service to the world. Rather, it is an attempt to reclaim the church's one foundation, to recover the bedrock upon which our lives and our ministries are built.

As I pondered this article, I asked myself two questions: (1) Why is it that more than sixteen thousand new Christians are added in Africa per day, while about six thousand church members in Europe and North America are lost to other religions or no religion daily? (2) How can I, as one Christian woman, and my church, as one among many, experience here in this place and time the energy and the wholehearted commitment that I've described in one church in Ghana and was certainly manifest in the New Testament church?

At this juncture, God caught me by surprise, as is so often the case.

I was reading the Book of Leviticus, and if I am honest, I was more or less reading to "get through it" when I came upon these words, or rather, these words came upon me: "The fire must be kept burning upon the altar continually; it must not go out" (6:13, NIV). I have been possessed by these words ever since, even though at this moment I don't quite understand why. I am convinced that herein lies a powerful and empowering message for the church in North America today. The words burn in my spirit. They will not leave me alone.

God's presence is associated throughout the Scriptures with fire. God had shown Moses that the Holy Presence was to be found in fire. According to the priestly school of the Israelites, the continuing fire on the altar was the same fire that had been sent by God to consume the first offering ever made—a divine act of grace, the gift of God's presence. God had initiated the fire. Now it was the responsibility of the covenant community, through their priests, to be the keepers of the fire—day and night, night and day, from generation to generation.

It is no surprise, then, that on the day of Pentecost the promised gift of the Holy Spirit that was to empower the followers of Jesus in their assigned task of continuing the witness he had begun came like tongues of fire. In contrast to the single burning fire upon the tabernacle altar, the tongues of fire separated and came to rest on each believer. Each was filled. Each began to prophesy.

The ever-burning altar fire symbolized obedience to the divine command that the covenant nation should worship God alone. It was a constant reminder to the Israelites of their need for continued worship and faithfulness to God; in turn, it assured them of God's constant vigilance on their behalf.

From the divine side, the fire represented the unceasing, uninterrupted character of God—a reminder of God's grace, yes, and also a reminder of divine judgment of sin and of God's purification of the sinner. Fire as the metaphor of God's holiness may destroy, purge, and inspire awe. It never leaves us comfortably alone.

The repeated refrain of Leviticus, "Be holy as I am holy," is the theme that unites the ethics of the Old and New Testaments. Holiness must find expression in holy living in the covenant community at worship and at work. It was God's expectation of the Israelites. It is God's expectation of us today.

God has always known that holy living is not possible in human strength alone. For this reason, God assured the Israelites that they would never be without God's abiding presence symbolized in the altar fire. In a much more life-giving, personal, and empowering way, Christ assured his followers that even though he was to leave them, they would never be alone. The gift and presence of God's Holy Spirit, indwelling each one of them and each one of us, is the distinctive feature of the new humanity that Christ came to inaugurate and put into motion. Only the gift of the Holy Spirit can make holy living possible. Only through the Spirit's power do we image God in the world. To image God is the calling of the Christian.

Is this what we have forgotten or at least suppressed? Could the quenching of the Spirit account for the indictment of the church by Wood's friend, "nothing is happening"? What of "burnout"? Is that the dying of the Spirit? Could this be what Leith refers to when he claims that much of our worship and much of our living fails to mediate the holy presence and grace of God—that we have lost our distinctive message? Possibly so. Somehow I see a connection between the command of God to Israel, "The fire on the altar must not go out," and the command in the New Testament text, "Do not put out the Spirit's fire."

As the Israelites were commanded that the fire must not go out, lest they forget who they were, today's Christians are subject to two commands, lest we forget who we are: (1) "Be filled with the Spirit" (Ephesians 5:18b, NIV), and (2) "Do not put out the Spirit's fire" (1 Thessalonians 5:19, NIV).

These two imperatives need to be heeded in our churches today. Here is the source of life-giving energy and joy that will move us individually and corporately from malaise to fullness of life. Until we tap the source, we will continue to minister out of moral oughtness, just like any other caring and sharing society.

The gift of the Spirit and the unique spiritual gifts with which each of us is endowed are both divine gifts of grace. As it was the responsibility of the Israelites to be keepers of the fire burning on the altar, our responsibility as the people of God in this time is two-fold: (1) individually, each of us is to be the keeper of the fire within, and (2) corporately, we are to be keepers of the fire within the congregation and the larger body of Christ in the world.

Our New Testament text contains five short, sharp commands that form a clearly bound unity, all of which relate to the presence of the Spirit. These commands or imperatives are essential fuel for keeping the fire burning.

1. *Be joyful always.* Express joy based on Christ and all that he has accomplished for us and for the whole human family. Joy is indeed a mark of the Christian life.

2. *Pray continually.* As a young Christian, I wondered how this could be possible. For me now, to pray continually is to live with an awareness of living all of life in the presence of God, upon whom I depend for all things. It calls me to make my work, my leisure, my pain, my joy an offering of worship. The I-Thou relationship is kept constantly alive via the dialogue of prayer made possible through Christ who always makes intercession for you and me.

3. *Give thanks in all circumstances.* Thanksgiving is the acknowledgement of a grateful heart that affirms that God in Christ is with us and provides for us in the full spectrum of the human experience. The loving, sustaining Presence never leaves us. What cause for thanksgiving!

4. *Do not put out the Spirit's fire.* To stifle or quench the fire is to grieve the Spirit by disregarding the Spirit's presence, refusing the Spirit's guidance, failing to listen to the Spirit's conviction of sin and call to repentance, and failing to receive the blessing that comes with the fullness of the Spirit. In this particular context, Paul is referring to the specific gifts of the Spirit found among the membership of the church. A major responsibility of any congregation is the calling out and affirmation of gifts—a stirring of the flame, the gifts of the Spirit in each member.

5. *Do not treat prophecy with contempt.* The primary function of prophecy is to declare the present will of God for the human family and the created order. A prophetic voice, then, is one that tells forth the will of God. The prophetic voice in our time is in great need of being rekindled, not suppressed.

Here we have what some have called "the standing orders of the church." I am calling these imperatives the fuel for those of us who are the keepers of the fire. Presented in these five imperatives is a

picture of the transformation that comes over human life when we are
"in Christ" by the supernatural power of the indwelling Spirit.

Who is the Holy Spirit?
The Holy Spirit is a compassionate
outpouring
of the Creator
and the Son.
This is why
when we on earth
pour out compassion and mercy
from the depths of our hearts
and give to the poor
and dedicate our bodies to the
service of the broken,
to that very extent
do we resemble the Holy Spirit.
—Mechtild of Magdeberg[3]

This is the way of life embodied for us in Christ and willed for us
by God. Is it possible? Only when we are faithful keepers of the fire.

When our churches are known for keeping these commands—rejoice; pray always; give thanks in all circumstances; keep the fire
burning; raise the prophetic voice—our churches will be vibrant with
contagious life. Much will happen. We ourselves will be surprised by
joy!

The proof that God raised Jesus
from the dead is not
the empty tomb,
but the full hearts
of his transformed disciples.

The crowning evidence that he lives
is not a vacant grave,
but a spirit-filled fellowship;
not a rolled-away stone,
but a carried-away church.
—Clarence Jordan[4]

This sermon was preached in April 1989 in Durham, North Carolina, at Watts Street Baptist Church.

NOTES

1. Ralph Wood, "The Business of the Church," *Christian Century* (March 1, 1989), 221-222.

2. John Leith, *The Reformed Imperative* (Philadelphia: Westminster Press, 1980), 22.

3. Reprinted from *Meditations with Mechtild of Magdeberg*, edited by Sue Woodruff, Copyright 1982, Bear & Co., Inc., P.O. Drawer 2860, Santa Fe, NM 87504. Page 117.

4. Clarence Jordan, *The Substance of Faith and Other Cotton Patch Sermons* (Americus, Ga.: Koinonia Partners, 1972), 29.

Woman Standing Straight

Luke 13:10-17

Lynda Weaver-Williams

Are you tired of hearing about 1992 being "The Year of the Woman"?

Indeed, as never before, women ran for and won political office. By January 1992 there will be six women in the Senate and forty-seven in the House. There will probably be even more women's faces around as the appointees in President-elect Clinton's administration are announced. For those who think that it makes sense to have women in the decision-making process of a country whose population majority is female, all this is good news.

As I watched the faces of some of the new senators and representatives last week, I recalled some other faces we have seen in the last year, some other women's faces whose lives are not unrelated to the year's political victories.

I remember the face of Anita Hill, who refused to sit down and be quiet, who refused to go along and get along. The face of Desiree Washington, who withstood not only Mike Tyson's unwelcome advances but also his invitation to take the money and run. The face of William Kennedy Smith's victim as she testified against him in his infamous Palm Beach rape trial. I remember their faces, faces that have been part of our collective history in the last year.

Now I realize that some of you are put off by my raising these women's names and faces: some of you think they are liars and opportunists, others of you are simply uncomfortable with the nature of their charges and the publicity surrounding them. But I place before you a striking possibility: simply because of what these women did—*stand up*—I think we are in a new place to hear the story from Luke today.

Whatever you believe about these women, they were at least willing to *stand up* and speak their truth. Everywhere they turned, somebody was attempting to silence them, to diminish them, to get them to simply sit down and be quiet. Oh, forget it, they said to Anita Hill; it happened so long ago. Forget it, they said to Desiree Washington; it only happened once. Forget it, they said to Willie Smith's victim, it happens all the time. Just let it go, girls; sit down and be quiet.

Now then, we come to this story about Jesus and a woman who had spent most of her life down and quiet. "She was bent over," says the text (Luke 13:11, RSV), unable to stand; for eighteen years she had been staring at feet, not faces. And Jesus gives her a freedom word: "Woman, you are freed from your infirmity" (Luke 13:12). This is a freedom word if ever there was one; it is a word worth hearing again.

This is not a story we often read. It is found only in the gospel of Luke. That's where we might expect to find it, and where we might expect to find it along side a companion story. Ever notice how Luke often pairs stories? Many times in this gospel there will be a story or parable about a woman like this one, and somewhere nearby is a similar story about a man. In Luke 15, we have the story of the patient father and prodigal son paired with the persistent widow searching for a coin. So we have a story about a woman who is shrunken in size and cannot fully straighten herself in Luke 13, paired with a passage in Luke 14 about a man who is so full of himself, so swollen with his own fluids, that he is disabled in another way. Leave it to Luke to accomplish gender balance and equal opportunity powerlessness!

The frame of our story is the sabbath controversy. Picture this: it is a proper sabbath setting. Jesus is teaching in the synagogue on the sabbath. Jesus is doing the right thing, in the right place, at the right time . . . but not for long.

He notices a woman. She didn't approach him. She didn't ask for anything. She didn't touch the hem of his garment. She didn't intrude; she was proper. She was doing the right thing as best she could. After all, she was a woman and didn't have full run of the synagogue. She was there, on the day of worship, the right place at the right time.

Jesus gives her a freedom word; a password of grace, "Woman, you are freed from your infirmity!" You are released. You can stand up full in the face of God. "Infirmity" is a fitting King James term in this story. It carries a portion of the meaning of this word, which is that there is the suggestion of something within, some kind of debilitating disease, perhaps, that has kept this woman looking at feet, not faces, for eighteen years. This word is also used in the New Testament to indicate an exterior burden, some pressure from without that holds one down, something that keeps you constantly bent over with the suffering of life, some burden that does not permit you to look people in the eye.

And so Jesus' words, "Woman you are freed from your infirmity," is the cure for what ails you from within and what burdens you from without. Stand up, woman; enough of feet, let's look at faces. Stand up and stretch the full length of your being.

Now I want you to stand up, right where you are, without really thinking. Just stand up. Now look at how you are standing. How much room are you taking up? Are your arms spread out or folded? Are your feet close together or planted wide? Are you taking up as little space as possible or as much as possible?

Often when men stand up, they take up as much room as possible, with head and shoulders held high, sometimes even an arm braced against their sides to extend their body space. Now, women often stand with their arms folded, sometimes with their shoulders hunched over and their feet close together to emphasize the small space they inhabit.

Take note of your positioning and now reverse it. If you are taking up a small amount of space, rearrange yourself to expand. If you are a maximum-space person, draw yourself in a little and position yourself in a smaller space. Many times when people try this, they begin to realize how they consciously connect how they stand to how they feel. Men often say that standing in a smaller space makes them feel less visible, less present to what is going on. Women often remark that maximizing the space around them feels odd at first; they feel exposed, but then they report that gradually they begin to feel more confident and strong.[1]

Now, once more: close your eyes and let your body gravitate to a position where it feels comfortable. There is a certain body knowledge that can guide us. You may sit down. The mere effort of standing up does speak to us in ways that are deeper than we know. The freedom word of Jesus, to the woman who could not stand, was freedom in more ways than one.

In *Teaching a Stone to Talk,* Annie Dillard recalls her research into polar expeditions. The most tragic and fascinating of these expeditions was the one charted by Sir John Franklin in 1845. He set out from England in the spring to find the northwest passage through the Canadian Arctic. This journey was outfitted in fine English style, with china place settings, cut glass wine goblets, and sterling silver flatware for the officers. Instead of extra coal to fire the ship's engines, they carried a twelve-hundred-volume library and a hand organ. For years after the expedition was lost, the Inuit Indians of the region kept finding bodies of the Franklin group. No one survived, but many of the would-be survivors were found frozen with their backpacks still in place. Inside they carried sterling silver flatware, backgammon pieces, and silk neckerchiefs, all proper items for English gentlemen.[2]

Every one of us is carrying around some sterling silver flatware, and it has us bent double. Just like the woman in the story, every one of us is burdened from without. We are all carrying some unnecessary baggage, some idealized concept of what a proper Christian is supposed to be or do or have. Every one of us is weighed down by expectations of family, friends, congregation, denomination, colleagues, or, most excruciating of all, our own standards. And this sterling silver flatware we're hauling is completely unnecessary for the journey of faith.

We need to lay it all down. Lay down all the useless notions of what a woman minister is supposed to do or what a male minister is supposed to achieve. Lay down how an average Christian is supposed to manage; what a wife or mother is supposed to be or what a husband or father is supposed to do; what a marriage or a ministry or a relationship is supposed to look like. We need to unload, unpack, empty all those illusions of where we thought we'd be at thirty or forty-five or sixty-two. We simply need to hear the freedom word of Jesus, "Women, men, you are freed from your infirmities." Friends, we are free.

Go back to the story and notice that Jesus didn't give this woman anything. He didn't tell her she had great faith or that her sins were forgiven or that she had chosen wisely. He simply empowered this woman to be what was in her to be. It was all already there: her muscles were ready to do their work, her nervous system set to go on line, her bones ready to rise to their heights. All the raw material was present. Jesus simply gave her the password to freedom.

You and I have within us the bone and muscle that makes for faith. We have the energy and the strength to stretch out in the fullness of grace. We have the deep, brooding intuitive spaces in us that can prompt us to stand up and speak up. It's all already there. We need to know it and to let ourselves be engaged by Jesus' freedom word. This thing we do called "a journey of faith" is really not about professional competency or academic degrees or certification or ordination or somebody sanctioning our lives.

In her novel *Beloved*, Toni Morrison draws a magnificent portrait of a slave woman turned free preacher. Baby Suggs preaches the freedom word of Jesus every summer Saturday to her congregation of runaway and freed slaves who steal away and meet her in the woods. This is what she tells them: "She did not tell them to clean up their lives or to go and sin no more. She did not tell them they were the blessed of the earth, its inheriting meek or its glory-bound pure. She told them that the only grace they could have was the grace they could imagine. That if they could not see it, they would not have it."[3]

Jesus didn't give the woman anything she didn't already have except a new way to be in the world. He gave to her the moment when she could stand straight and tall, the moment when she could reveal her face and straighten her spine, when she could look everyone else level in the eye. He gave to her a moment of grace she had been imagining every back-breaking day of her life. He gave her a new worldview: a world of faces, not feet.

What new worldview do you suppose we might have if grace was imagined in our lives? How many more straight-standing women and men might there be if we introduced our imaginations to divine grace?

There will always be people hanging around the synagogue ready to denounce any show of grace. There will always be somebody who gets bent out of shape over someone else's freedom. And there will always be someone who announces "Woman (or women), sit down and be quiet." There will always be people who don't want to hear Jesus' freedom word for themselves or for any of the rest of us.

We need not be deterred. Jesus wasn't. For we are the ones who have heard the message. We have unearthed the story and seen the face of a woman who had not known freedom for eighteen years. We have witnessed the word: "Woman, man—indeed, friends—we are freed from all our infirmities." We cannot walk away unchanged! Our straight spines, our grace-giving hearts compel us to walk from this place and know we are the ones for whom we've been waiting. Indeed, perhaps we are even the ones for whom the world has been waiting!

This sermon was preached November 9, 1992, at the Virginia Baptist Pastors Conference.

Reprinted by permission from LYDIA'S CLOTH: a worship resource written by women. Vol. 2, 5, Sept.-Oct., 1992. Lydia's Cloth, 590 Amanda Lane, Fallon, Nevada 89406.

NOTES

1. Based on an exercise in Gloria Steinem's *Revolution from Within* (New York: Little, Brown & Co., 1992), 199.
2. Annie Dillard, *Teaching a Stone to Talk* (New York: Harper & Row Publishers, Inc., 1982), 24-26.
3. Toni Morrison, *Beloved* (New York: Plume Publishing, 1987), 107.

The Whisper of God

1 Kings 19:9-12

Leigh Q. Moseman

To ensure the worship of the god Baal, Jezebel, the wife of King Ahab of Israel, had the prophets of Yahweh killed. The only prophet of God left, Elijah, goes to the Northern Kingdom of Israel to bring the people back to a true covenant relationship.

In an amazing display of confidence, Elijah calls the people of Israel and the prophets of Baal to Mount Carmel. In words reminiscent of Joshua, he essentially tells the people to "choose this day whom ye will serve." To understand the people's hesitancy, we need to remember that all the other prophets of God had been killed. The people decide to wait to see what will happen, which is conveyed in the words: "The people did not answer him a word" (1 Kings 18:21). They would never have imagined what was about to occur.

Elijah challenges the prophets of Baal, declaring that the God who answers by fire will be the true God. The prophets of Baal build their altar and pray all day to Baal. There is no response. With twelve stones, Elijah builds an altar in the name of Yahweh. He places a sacrificial bull upon the wood. To the surprise of the gathering, he then makes a trench around the altar and pours water on the altar, soaking the wood and the bull and filling the trench. Elijah then prays to God, "LORD God . . . , let it be known this day that you are God in Israel. Answer me, O LORD, answer me, so that this people may know that you, O LORD, are God" (1 Kings 18:36-37).

The fire of the Lord fell and consumed the altar, the wood, the bull, and the water in the trench. In response, the people fell on their faces in worship to the true God. Elijah bowed and praised God for the victory at Mount Carmel, and Yahweh blesses the people by sending rain to the drought-stricken land.

Yet, the celebration ends quickly when Elijah receives word that Jezebel has vowed to kill him. We are told that "the hand of the Lord came upon Elijah" and he flees to the city of Beersheba. He has been faithful to the work of God, and his life is now in danger. Seeking solitude and a chance to pour out his weariness to God, Elijah continues his flight into the desert.

Sitting under a juniper tree, physically and spiritually exhausted, he no longer desires to live. He begins to pray and asks to die. He then falls asleep. An angel comes and cares for his needs by providing food and water. After he rests for a while, the angel comes once again to give Elijah more nourishment, for he is about to travel forty days and nights to a mountain named Horeb, the mountain of God.

In 1 Kings 19:9-12, we are told Elijah "came to a cave, and spent the night there. Then the word of the Lord came to him, saying, 'What are you doing here, Elijah?' He answered, 'I have been very zealous for the LORD, the God of hosts; for the Israelites have forsaken your covenant, thrown down your altars, and killed your prophets with the sword. I alone am left; and they are seeking my life, to take it away.'"

God leads Elijah to the mouth of the cave, and a strong wind comes with such force that it breaks rocks from the mountain. Then an earthquake and fire descend. As the world around him is shaking and exploding, I imagine Elijah is simply trying to survive the storm. God was not in the wind. God was not in the earthquake. God was not in the fire. We wonder, where was God? And after the fire came the still, small voice.

I was very athletic as a youngster and teenager. After winning a game, when the team would be discussing going to celebrate at the local Dairy Queen, I only wanted to go home and lie down because my legs hurt so badly. Of course, I said nothing and enjoyed my ice cream along with everyone else. When the pain became worse, I finally mentioned it to my parents. Over the next few years, we saw many doctors and were told it must be growing pains or a slight scoliosis (curvature of the spine).

Even when I limited my activity, I knew my condition deteriorated as the pain and numbness in my legs increased. One day, while at college, my legs collapsed. I was admitted to a hospital and was diagnosed with a condition that affected a vertebra in my lower back. Due to not being diagnosed earlier, I had sustained permanent nerve damage to the sciatic nerve to my legs. Following two back surgeries, I began the long road of rehabilitation and healing. My father had retired by this time and so was home with me. My mother was working as a special education teacher. Although I was still weak, I was thankful that I was walking with assistance. One evening, my dad said he wondered if I had become content with my progress instead of discontent with my remaining limitations. He felt that if I kept working, I could eventually walk without any assistance. I casually shrugged because I was thankful to be home and to have a break from physical therapy.

I awoke one morning and could hear the television in the den. I called to my father to bring my crutches. He responded that I could make it without them. I struggled up and even took a few steps. I was still weak and soon decided I didn't desperately need to go to the bathroom, so I returned to bed for a few more hours of sleep. When I awoke, I again asked my dad to bring my crutches. He said that I could make it. I couldn't believe this man. Didn't he realize all I had been through? More furious with each step, I made it halfway down the hall and withered to the floor. I began to yell at him, eventually crying myself into exhaustion. I awoke hours later and found that I had been gently tucked into bed.

Needless to say, when my mother got home, I began to cry. I asked her to stay home with me. I could hear only the muffled sounds of my parent's conversation and my mother crying. Later, trying to encourage me, she explained that Daddy was doing what he felt was best for me. I was not happy.

Each day the pattern continued. As I held onto the wall, I could see the back of his head as he sat in the recliner in the den. When he would offer help, I refused his arm.

Progress was evident as I made it to the bathroom, the den, and then to the table. Oh, it was a marvelous day for us all when I walked through the pasture to the pond. I had waited and worked a long time to make it to my favorite place.

About a year later, my dad and I were sitting on the tailgate of the jeep, shucking corn and reminiscing. I told Daddy how much I loved him and thanked him for helping me in my recovery. Tears streamed down his face. He said that hearing me struggle with each step, seeing me angry, and feeling the distance between us were the hardest days of his life. I had not known that he too had been crying as he sat grasping the arms of his chair, praying to God.

The storms of our lives often rage as much on the inside as they do on the outside. Each of us has experienced the pains and storms of life. We have felt the mighty winds. Knocked down by financial difficulties or the stress at work or home, we struggle to stand.

Due to the sickness and death of a loved one, the earthquakes have destroyed life as we knew it. Previously a strong foundation of love, security, and joy, the ground beneath our feet is crumbling. We do not know if our hearts or our lives will ever heal. We search for stability and answers.

For some, due to divorce, broken promises, and painful verbal exchanges, anger has consumed us. Our attitude and witness have been burned on the altar of hatred and grief. For those of us who have faced a serious physical illness, pain does feel like fire that burns so deeply within that it is sometimes hard to sleep or even breathe. Thus, during the wind, the earthquake, and the fire of life, we have fought and screamed. We have searched for God.

Elijah was searching. He had given his life to God and he had been a good servant. Through his feelings of abandonment and despair, God was ever present, always providing for Elijah's needs. The hand of the Lord led him to safety from the threat of Jezebel. The angel came twice to provide food and water.

During the storms of our lives, God is always with us. There are times when God is walking alongside. Times when we are encouraged to go as far as we can. Times when we crumble to the floor exhausted, only to find hours later that we have been picked up and gently tucked into bed to rest and regain our strength. Times when we are so angry that when God reaches out to help us, we say, "Leave me alone. I don't want or need your help." Times when God can only sit grasping the arms of the chair, praying through tears for us.

"Yea, though I walk through the valley of the shadow of death, I will fear no evil: for Thou art with me" (Psalm 23:4, KJV). God has kept the promise to never leave nor forsake us. The problem for many of us is that we have left and forsaken God. Our hearts are so cluttered by selfishness, pride, anger, and worldly desires that we do not even hear the voice, the delicate whisper, of God. We have no trouble hearing God through the loud trumpet blasts, but how easily we can miss the still, small voice. We must be prepared to experience God. We must "be still" in order to "know" that thou art God (Psalm 46:1, KJV). We must stand at the mouth of the cave, always watching and listening for God's voice.

Yes, Elijah wanted to turn and run and die; but he waited, he watched, and he listened. Elijah heard the voice of God, a voice that knew Elijah's despair. A voice that offered strength and renewed hope to lead him to descend from the mountain and to continue the work of God.

Let us go with him.

Preached on Father's Day, June 1993, at Hardwick Baptist Church, Hardwick, Georgia.

A Large Table

1 Chronicles 16:23-34; Acts 2:42-47

Molly Marshall

I must confess that I am a fairly regular devotee of Miss Manners's column on etiquette. This witty writer tells us that many contemporary persons feel unprepared to negotiate the daunting task of negotiating table manners—the line-up of forks and spoons can send even the most high-powered corporate officer into a frenzy of incompetence. There is something about eating that brings out the best and worst in us. We are either at our hospitable best or are most noticeably exclusive. In his commentary on Acts, William Willimon tells us, "We know, from contemporary experience, that social boundaries between persons are often most rigidly enforced at the table."[1]

Our New Testament lesson outlines the Jerusalem Christian community's embodiment of the gospel. The marks of their new relationship in Christ were distinctive: they were devoted to the apostles' teaching; they expressed their loving partnership in material ways; they regularly engaged in "the breaking of bread" with glad and generous hearts; and they kept the spiritual discipline of corporate prayer. Today we focus on the breaking of bread.

As a child of about seven, I made a wonderful discovery one Sunday evening as we celebrated the Lord's Supper. I realized that there were two sides to our altar table. I was used to seeing the side that read "Bring Ye All the Tithes into the Storehouse" as the deacons set the offering plates on the table at each service. That particular evening, however, I noticed that the table also bore another inscription: "Do This in Remembrance of Me." Thus, the first aspect of my eucharistic theology was formed: we do this in memory of Jesus.

It was many more years before I realized that we do this in remembrance of others as well. We celebrate this meal with all of God's faithful, "in mystic sweet communion with those whose rest is won"[2] as well as with those who, on this day, share our confession of Christ as the Bread of the World, in mercy broken. Can we even begin to imagine all the forms "the breaking of bread" will take on World Communion Sunday, as Christ's body celebrates communion with him and with one another? In south Florida a congregation whose small church was blown away by Hurricane Andrew celebrates in their homes, as a part of a potluck dinner, and remembers the lives taken by the hurricane. The faithful in Russia will remember those who continued to offer thanksgiving for Christ's body when it was not welcome by the state. Arab Christians in East Jerusalem will think about the almost insuperable barriers that exist between them and the "completed Jews" who worship not too many kilometers to the West.

We also remember those for whom no place is set at any table. They are the famine-stricken who have never seen a table; they are the forgotten who never make it onto the guest list; they are the lonely who find community only in the neighborhood bar; they are those who at one time gathered with Christ's church but now suffer "eucharistic famine," as Rosemary Ruether has said, because of the church's social boundaries.

When we pray "give us today our daily bread," we need also to pray for the conviction of will "to give them their daily bread." To give bread is to give ourselves; as you recall when the disciples asked Jesus to send the crowds away so that they might purchase what they needed for their daily bread, he countered their suggestion with "you feed them." He was asking them to find a way to put a leaf in their table, to expand their understanding of the manner of God's hosting of hungry humanity.

Eating together is a mark of unity, solidarity, and deep friendship. When a student in England, I was amazed that strangers could sit at the same table, to save space, and never utter a word. To share only a table without sharing conversation, virtually ignoring the presence of another, seems a violation of all that mealtime was meant to be. We know that a meal holds both promise and threat. It makes us nervous to eat with someone we hardly know, and yet laughter and conversation around a table is a wonderful opportunity to enter the life of others in a meaningful way.

The early Christian communities knew of Jesus' reputation as a "glutton and winebibber"—or at least as one who enjoyed eating with all sorts of people. Jesus risked God's reputation regularly—or at least his own—by his table manners! It seems that he did not wait for persons to repent before he had table fellowship with them. More often than not, it was his compassionate acceptance of sinners prior to their confession of faith in him that prompted them to believe in him. In his work *Jesus: A New Vision*, Marcus Borg writes, "It must have been an extraordinary experience for an outcast to be invited to share a meal with a man who was rumored to be a prophet." Thus, his acceptance of them, as Borg says, "would have been perceived as a claim that they were accepted by God."[3] This was quite different from the common Pharisee practice of social and religious ostracism from the table. To refuse to share a meal symbolized disapproval and rejection.

The early church linked eucharistic celebration to regular mealtime. In wisdom they understood the connection between food on the table and God's love for the world demonstrated in Christ crucified. The fact that persons daily were being added to their fellowship indicates that they were making this connection clear by the grace of Christian hospitality and their care for those in need.

We would do well to reclaim this essential connection. How can we partake of Christ's broken body and spilt blood and forget all those for whom Christ also died? It may be that our table is too small, its edges too sharp, for others to hear our nearly inaudible invitation. Perhaps we cannot share eucharistic fellowship with glad and generous hearts at Christ's table until we learn to put our feet under the same table with those whom we count as strangers in this world.

How then can we "devote ourselves to the breaking of bread"? One way is by becoming more intentional in recognizing every meal as an opportunity to recognize Jesus "in the breaking of the bread," a favorite theme of Luke. The common humanity we can discover with those who seem so very different from us puts us in touch with our common hunger for acceptance and grace. With whom do we eat? It says a great deal about us, you know.

We have not yet fully taken hold of Jesus' promise that "many will come from east and west and sit at table with Abraham, Isaac, and Jacob in the kingdom of heaven . . ." (Matthew 8:11, RSV). "Close" communion, as Landmark Baptists[4] put it, has really meant "closed communion" at our family tables and at Christ's table. Although we do not share their narrow view of Baptist ecclesiology, we have often functioned in their exclusive manner.

As we share this meal as the gathered community of faith in this place, let us remember the One who gave himself for us; let us remember those who have everywhere and at all times celebrated his life, death, and resurrection in this manner; and let us remember those who are not here and find ways to include them in our lives and the life of Christ's body gathered at the table. Amen.

This sermon was preached on World Communion Sunday, October 4, 1992, at Crescent Hill Baptist Church in Louisville, Kentucky.

NOTES

1. William Willimon, *Acts*, Interpretation Series (Atlanta: John Knox Press, 1988).

2. From "The Church's One Foundation," by Samuel Wesley.

3. Marcus Borg, *Jesus: A New Vision* (San Francisco: Harper & Row, 1987), 101-102.

4. Landmarkism: "A term used to denominate a Southern Baptist party which developed considerable strength and influence in the nineteenth century. The distinctive tenets center on the primacy of the local church, exclusivism, and the 'true' church." —W. Morgan Patterson, *Encyclopedia of Southern Baptists* (Nashville: Broadman Press, 1958), 757.

Freedom from Within

2 Timothy 1:6-7

Nancy Ellett Allison

Some still question my sanity. I was once possessed. I had seven unclean spirits who racked my body. I was completely unclean. Mary of Magdala—the woman to avoid. But that was before I met the Christ.

> *Rabbi, heal me. You alone can free me from my pain.*
> *Rabbi, touch me. Can you free me from my shame?*
> *Rabbi, forgive me. Free me from despair.*

Once I was shamed, now I know love. Once I despaired, now I rejoice. Once I was shunned and silenced, now I can proclaim!

> *I proclaim a Christ risen and free!*
> *Free to touch and teach the unclean . . .*
> *Free to sit with sinners . . .*
> *Free to celebrate with new wine at weddings . . .*
> *Free to act for each of us in love . . .*
> *I proclaim Christ!*

And now I'm no longer called unclean—but I am challenged for my witness. But how could I not speak of God's redeeming power? How could I not tell my story of a new life, a life beyond restrictions?

I was terrified the morning of Christ's resurrection. But my Redeemer said, "Go. Tell what you have seen." And so it is Christ I proclaim; and if I am challenged, so be it. I have nothing to lose, and only Christ to gain.

Could those have been some of Mary Magdalene's feelings in those early days of Resurrection and Pentecost, those days of new horizons and exciting possibilities, when her freedom sounded like craziness and the Spirit's moving looked like drunkenness? Mary's freedom from her old fears incarnated the admonition Paul gave young Timothy. Listen to this passage from 2 Timothy 1:6-7:

Rekindle the gift of God that is in you . . . for God did not give us a spirit of fear but a spirit of power, and of love, and of self-discipline (author's paraphrase).

Timothy's challenge and Mary's untethered witness can model for us how to live with abandon as Spirit-filled, loving disciples.

It is courage and freedom that enable us to live outside the constraints of religious expectation, like Mary the proclaimer. However, a spirit of fear too often keeps us bound.

The unpredictable, the uncontrollable, the unknown—these are our fears. We long for control, conventionality, and certainty. Free thought is suppressed. Diversity is eliminated. The future is prescribed.

Listen again. The unpredictable: God saying to Job, "Does the rain have a father? Who fathers the drops of dew? From whose womb comes the ice? Who gives birth to the frost from the heavens?" (Job 38:28-29, author's translation). The uncontrollable: God, a raging spirit of fire. The unknown: I Am Who I Am.

When we walk in to our fears, we walk in with God. Oh, but the tension of living fully in God's presence! How much easier it is to accept the immediate gratification of compromise than to live with the tension of relating to an uncontrollable God. The promise of God is not security. It is life—abundant, free, risk-taking life! If we are to find life, we must learn to move into and not away from our fears.

I met a man nine years ago who loves Africa. He came alive when he talked about his friends in Zimbabwe. He thought he might go back someday. Not me! I was real happy ministering in North Dallas, the home of immediate gratification and compromise. I was not called of God into that great African unknown. I certainly did like and respect this guy; so we talked. In his company I learned about life overseas; and in God's company I struggled with my fears. I spent a summer in agony. I had never wanted to be a missionary. Could I say yes to any call from God? Was I that free? That faithful? What if I didn't like those people? What if they didn't like me? I had a lot to lose! I had every intention of controlling my future, but I allowed one man's fascinating, fearless stories of God's reality in his African experience to make an impact. We married. Spirit spoke to spirit. God's power moved in me, and I was transformed into a less-than-legendary missionary to Africa.

What fears are raised for you in this company of the committed? What aspect of risk-taking life lies in front of you? Walk into your anxiety with someone who understands. Call upon our uncontrollable God to carry you tenderly into the unknown.

We have not been given "a spirit of fear but a spirit of power, of love, and of self-discipline." What does a God-given spirit of power look like? God's spirit of power is life-changing from within. Power is the ability to direct another's behavior or an entire group's actions. I can still make my four-year-old brush her teeth. The law says you can't shout, "fire!" in this room. These are external controls.

God's Spirit of power begins in love and works from within. When love is recognized, our faith is kindled and experienced as hope. Courageous hope becomes our way of living. Mary Magdalene's intense encounter with Christ charged her faith, crystalized hope and courage, and made her the most important proclaimer of the Resurrection. She affected the behavior of others. A free woman. A faithful disciple.

We know a lot about love. We talk about it all the time. We live too little in love. Why is that? The Apostle John claims that perfect love casts out fear, but is one of our great fears love? Love—like God—cannot be controlled. I can't make you love me. We can't stop God from loving us.

If we are love's source, it can never be greater than our own limits and satisfactions. I love you as you please me. Paul promises God's Spirit of love. Receiving this love, we can become a conduit for a love greater than we are, a love not under our control and limits, a love that changes us in the midst of life.

A child is born. Parents are thrilled. There are immediate surges of love and pride. They respond to daily needs, but it is work. It's constant. It interferes with what was. Love discovers limits. The child grows. The parents respond. And one day—joy of joys—they discover that tasks reduced to duty are now done once again out of a love that now springs from a transformed nature. Experiencing God's liberating love also lifts us from commandment to fulfillment. What was once external command is now our greatest desire; and therein lies the risk: free-flowing love can be rejected. You can refuse my heart's offerings. You can reject my gifts. Only if we are empowered and sustained by God's Spirit will we commit to a life of love.

For full spiritual empowerment, we must yoke our love with self-discipline. To give self-discipline a nineties spin, we could talk about character formation. How are we shaped and made whole? By finding ourselves in God. Only in God's care can I accept myself "as is." Only in God's strength can I find myself in relation to you. Only in God's service can I discover my spiritual gifts. If we take seriously biblical teachings about the charismata, we discover most fully who we are.

Full formation of my character before God reveals the singularity of who I am. Knowing fully who I am distinguishes me all the more clearly from you. My gifts of teaching and leadership suit me as your gifts of mercy, or interpretation, or giving illumine you. It is these gifted differences that we must learn to value in each other. Christ's body is not fully formed if any are excluded.

Full formation of character, self-discipline before God, brings courageous anticipation and vitality to all our actions. Knowing ourselves makes our liberation real and future-oriented. Our faith is expressed in freedom.

The illumination we receive from God's Word gives us a transformed vision—not a vision of another world but a new vision of this real and valuable world. It is in this new world with no borders and ever-expanding horizons that we are challenged to live and proclaim today. It is working together for the rekindled vision of this new world that will keep us united.

As souls through the centuries have rekindled the gift of God in them and found their freedom from within, they have often been treated like people possessed: Mary Magdala, Francis of Assisi, Joan of Arc, Ulrich Zwingli, Sojourner Truth, and Martin Luther King, Jr.

As we return to our homes, let us be fearless, full of God's power,

love, and self-discipline, willing to risk all—even appearing possessed
for the proclamation of Christ risen and free!

*This sermon was preached in May 1992 at the Cooperative Baptist
Fellowship meeting in Birmingham, Alabama.*

Grace during Meals

Luke 10:38-42

Sharlande Sledge

The energetic, gregarious cook, Jeff Smith, known to television viewers as the "frugal gourmet," bases his economics of food preparation on the philosophy that "you use everything and are careful with your time as well as your food." Another important "doctrine" of his "frugal theology" is that one should spare no expense, provide nothing but the best, for loved ones. For Smith, preparing and sharing food is a sacred community event. Approaching the meal in an attitude of celebration transforms the mundane into the grace-filled. An ordinary meal becomes a time of thanksgiving.

> *"One expresses thanks for food," says Smith, "not because one is happy with the food. That's bad theology. That would mean that you would pray over a beautiful prime rib and Yorkshire pudding, but not over macaroni and cheese. That's cheap theology! We pray to give thanks for the fact that each time we sit down we realize again we are totally dependent upon God. . . . The initial blessing and our continued attitude during the meal come as acts of confession." Smith confesses: "I am able to eat, able to live, because God declared so."* [1]

In thanksgiving, in praise, in blessing, the prayers we offer at our meals often grow from carefully practiced traditions as much as from spontaneous feelings. Our customs vary from table to table: holding hands to form a circle, giving a quick squeeze when the "amen" is pronounced, singing the Doxology or the "Johnny Appleseed song," taking turns voicing prayers for those in need, saying the blessing at the end of a meal so that the tastes of the food may give voice to a fuller expression of thanks.

Lest you think that all grace-giving is done in reverence and decorum—hands folded, heads bowed, eyes closed—let me remind you that in reaching for the hand across the table, an iced tea glass is sometimes overturned. Thanks are often rushed, the meaning of the words lost in the hurry to eat before the pizza gets cold. Sometimes the question of *who* will pray takes more time than the table grace itself. Undue attention to correct manners and steaming food pushes God away from our table . . . if indeed we pause to sit down together at all. Fast prayers for fast food. We don't linger long enough to truly acknowledge God's generosity.

For whatever reason a table blessing is remembered, it provides a thoughtful gap in our tight schedules where God can conceivably intrude. We refer to it as "grace," after all. Strange that we can get so caught up in rituals and propriety that we forget the One who graces our table with both the physical provisions we need for our bodies and the spiritual presence we need for our souls. The One to whom we say "grace" before meals *is* Grace during meals.

Details. Details. Hurry-scurry. The to-do list in Martha's head took her far away from her pot of broth and lentils. Peeling, chopping, cutting, mincing, slicing, pouring, stirring, simmering, turning, frying, serving—her life was all motion, all process, all doing. If she were going to have a life with God, then God would have to run to catch up with her!

On the afternoon that Jesus was a guest in her home, Martha's anxiety about the correctness of a meal reached an all-time high. She wanted Jesus sufficiently impressed. Her nervousness, coupled with her tiredness, gave way to irritation, and this irritation became focused on her sister, Mary. "Lord, do you not care that my sister has left me to serve alone?" She asked. "Tell her then to help me" (Luke 10:40, RSV).

Imagine the silence in the room as the words left Martha's lips—the disciples, stopping mid-sentence to hear their Lord's reaction; Mary, perturbed that she might not hear the end of a story; the look in Jesus' eyes adding another layer of meaning to his response. "Martha, Martha, you are anxious and troubled about many things; one thing is needful. Mary has chosen the good portion, which shall not be taken away from her" (Luke 10:41-42, RSV).

That's all we know of the story as Luke records it. We do know that the Hebrew people did not lightly break bread together. In Jewish time, prayers were designated for use before, during, and after every meal. Eating was a sacred ritual. So that the vastness of God's gift of good land and the food harvested from it could be more fully appreciated, the host studied each dish as it was set on the table. Then he began the blessing: "Blessed art thou, O Lord our God, King of the universe . . ." With his mind's eye first on the loaf of bread, he continued, ". . . who brought forth bread from the earth . . ." Then for the pot of lentils he prayed, ". . . who created different kinds of seeds," and for the plate of onions and radishes, ". . . who created different kinds of herbs." "For the locusts, for the honey, for the bowl of fish, for the wine, for the baked fish." Each item of food and drink appropriately blessed, the host concluded, "For all came into existence by God's word. Amen." The host then raised his head, broke a loaf of bread, and distributed portions of food to each person at the table. Finally, everyone ate. The table around which the people gathered in the first century Hebrew home had God's fingerprints all over it.

What we know about Mary and Martha and Jesus tells us that a large measure of grace was served that night along with the bread and soup. For the one who reclined to eat in his "home away from home" saw the worth in each friend and recognized their unique gifts. He knew that the table spread Martha offered would be bland and tasteless without the salt of Mary's table talk; that hospitality consists as much of warm spirit as warm bread; that friendship is as dependent on intimate conversations as it is on group gatherings; and that companionship with God is as possible as serving God. What each one gave, Christ blessed, for the Giver of grace was present at their table that night.

How sure Martha must have been of her Lord's friendship that she could ask, "Do you not care that my sister has left me to do all the work by myself? Do you not care?"

Oh, Martha, Martha, you were worried about many things—the rising of the bread, the taste of the wine, the setting of the table. What you did not realize was that he *did* care. He cared so much that he offered himself as a gift of grace for you—and for us— so that we can be served bread and wine at the table over and over again. No, Martha, you did not deserve this blessing, but somehow you have it. Enjoy Christ as a guest at your table and understand that this One passing the cup to you is the Giver of all that matters. And this same One, Jesus Christ, can be a guest in your home without everything being perfect, for his presence offers an atmosphere of grace that says elbows on the table and spilled milk are O.K. Maybe the fact that the bread is too tough to tear is less important than the fact that there is bread to share. Smaller portions for those people around the table simply mean that there are more people around the table! Lingering conversation in the other room is not a lack of interest in tasting the soup but a time of nourishing one's spiritual appetite for a meal only enhanced by food.

It is grace that invites Mary and Martha and you and me to the table, and grace feeds us during the meal. So listen! Listen all you who have ears to hear! Stop! Stop whatever you are doing to come to the table.

And bring someone with you when you come—your sister, your brother, your parent, your child; the colleague who feels the push and pull of people and programs and cannot rest in Christ's presence; the parents of children living in poverty who wish as much as you to give good gifts to their children; the one so close to you that the familiarity of habits and behaviors cloud the need for new kinds of nourishment.

Let us join in recognizing the Lord in our midst. For the meal that Mary and Martha knew as tradition we now know as the body and blood of Christ, given for us. The Word made flesh who dwelled among them as Friend at their supper table in Bethany is now fully revealed to us through Christ's presence in our lives.

So come as you are; no need to rush about in preparation. No need to worry whether you have done enough. The blessing of table grace lasts throughout the meal, being transformed through Christ's presence into benediction, so that you may go into the world to make Christ known. Thanks be to God for this unspeakable gift!

This sermon was preached October 1992 as part of the Broadway Convocation series held at Broadway Baptist Church, Fort Worth, Texas.

NOTES

1. Pamela Payne Allen, "Feasting on Herbs in the Midst of Love: A Conversation with Jeff Smith," *The Christian Century* (December 2, 1987), 1087-1090.

Where Have All the Heroes Gone?

Exodus—Deuteronomy

Nancy Hastings Sehested

Heroes. Do you have any? Can you name one? Ted Turner was *Time* magazine's "Man of the Year." Is this the best we can do these days for heroes?

Heroes. Who needs 'em anyway? They'll just disappoint you in time. Where have all the heroes gone? Well, if you ever thought that John F. Kennedy was a hero, the latest revelations about him will get him off your list. And I guess you knew that one of the greatest heroes of the Constitution, Thomas Jefferson, who gave us the line "We hold these truths to be self-evident, that all men are created equal," forgot to mention women or the fact that he was a slave owner at the time of writing. Martin Luther, our Protestant Reformation hero, was the one who called marriage "an emergency hospital for the illness of human drives."

Where have all the heroes gone? Martin Luther King, Jr., has enough dirt out on him now to create another Mud Island in Memphis. Father Abraham of the faith had a mistress. Jacob was a manipulator. Moses was a murderer. King David was a womanizer. And even Jesus did not treat that Syro-Phoenician woman with much kindness. And he did not bring peace on earth, goodwill to all people.

It's hard to find good heroes anymore. Most of our heroes are fallen. In our day, if you are a hero, and you live long enough, you will be able to see your name dragged through every pothole you ever sunk into in your life. And if you die before that happens, then historians and journalists will do their best to drudge up all the gory details of your life for microscopic examination. Heroes don't stay heroes very long in this country. Wounded heroes are especially vulnerable prey for swarming vultures of the media . . . all done in the name of the search for the "real truth."

Heroes. Who needs them anyway? Well, I do. Don't you? I need heroes who know how to give themselves over to something bigger than they are. I need heroes who faithfully offer hope even when all signs have gone. Where have all the heroes gone?

The biblical heroes give me the best clues for what goes into making a hero. The Bible never even tries to pretty up the story of the people of God. The biblical heroes were ordinary, even ornery. Often they were unsure of themselves, and frequently they resisted doing great things for God. Most of them were reluctant heroes. But there was something so important about them that their stories—flaws and all—were saved, so that we might be saved from idol-making. At their best, they did give themselves over to be instruments for God—rough edges and all.

Moses was a reluctant hero if there ever was one. His life began in tears. The River Nile was flooded with the tears of Hebrew parents whose baby sons had been killed by a tyrannical pharaoh. His cries saved him from the bulrushes. He grew up in prosperity and privilege in the house of Pharaoh. Yet something in him from his precarious and perilous birth never died in him. As an adult he saw the forced labor of his people and his tears jumped to anger, which made its way to its fast end—violence. Moses became a murderer and had to flee to Midian when Pharaoh got wind of his act.

Overnight he went from the privilege of the palace to the fear and insecurity of a refugee. Moses settled into a life of shepherding in Midian. Then came the voice—right out of a burning bush: God wanted Moses to be the one to lead the Hebrew people to freedom. God wanted to ignite that smoldering fire in Moses' bones that knew how to burn against injustice.

Moses refused. Why me? Why not an angel? Why not my older brother Aaron? Why not someone without a stutter? Why not some-one single, without kids? Why not someone independently wealthy? Why not someone who likes to be an outside agitator? Why not someone who has the clothes for success? Besides, who am I going to say sent me?

Moses didn't want to go. He didn't want to break open those old wounds that had not healed yet; he didn't want to risk his life; he did not want any more rejection and disappointment in his life. But in the end, Moses said yes to God. God does like to win, you know. God does like to have the last word.

With Moses' yes, events started happening at a dizzying pace. Moses left the desert and took a front-row seat to the tumbling disintegration of an empire. Moses made plea after plea to Pharaoh to let the Hebrew people go. Moses kept pleading. Pharaoh wouldn't negotiate. A peace treaty was not signed. The methods changed—curses were uttered; plagues were called down; the angel of death appeared.

Then escape to the wilderness. The whole bunch of 'em marched out. When they got to the Red Sea, Moses shouted every step of the way. "Move on. Don't be afraid. Go into the water! Go on through it! Hurry! Hurry! Hurry!" Moses saw the questions in their eyes, wondering if they should've given Pharaoh one more chance. Moses directed them on. And they made it to the other side to freedom. They sang the "Hallelujah Chorus."

But it was the last time that song was heard through the forty years of wandering that followed. The rest of the time, the top-ten desert-wandering hit tunes were the blues. Too little water; too little food; too little shelter. Did God love them at all to send them out here to nothing? Moses spent forty years with too many complaints, too little help—and never enough resources.

Forty years and he still had not made it. Now, his life, which started in tears, was ending in tears. He had dreamed of lifting up a people from slavery—inspiring them, transforming them from paupers to princes. He had dreamed of creating a community of free men and women. But the Hebrews had fallen into the quicksand of in-fighting and complaining. Moses had pointed to God's work all around them; the freed slaves looked and saw nothing. Their lists of wants and demands grew longer. The runaway slaves had been witness to God's miracles of the Red Sea and the manna, of laws for just living, and now the water from rocks.

Moses grew angry and struck out. He'd handled so much alone. He'd been inundated with problems. He'd seen so much sorrow. Now, the one promise that had propelled Moses—the promise of the Promised Land—was gone. Over. He would die without going in; he could only have a good, long look over to the Land of Promise, but he could not go.

What kind of hero dies before the final triumphant scene? What kind of hero dies before the final scene of conquest and victory? God's kind of hero, that's who. Moses died. Martin Luther King, Jr., died. Jesus died.

"The people of Israel wept for Moses in the plains of Moab thirty days; then the days of weeping and mourning for Moses were ended" (Deuteronomy 34:8, RSV). And the people moved on toward the Promised Land. The people were tempted to make him into an idol. The people finally saw some of Moses' good and courageous leadership abilities. They were tempted to build a museum on the site of his death. But the people moved on into the Promised Land. The people considered building a temple around the burial site and charging admission to see the Ten Commandments. But the people moved on toward the Promised Land, and the place of burial was forgotten.

Heroes die. They all do—sooner or later. While they're alive, they usually stir up enough controversy that we wish they were dead—or we at least wish we could deny ever having been on their side.

Moses died. He was a hero. He died, perhaps one of the saddest and loneliest of leaders, but a powerful leader . . . the great prophet of Israel—or so the Bible tells us. No one knows where Moses' burial site is located. It was left unmarked. But the people were marked; they lived with his mark on their hearts. Wherever there is an injustice to be resisted, Moses lives on through them. Wherever there is a word of God's faith to be proclaimed, Moses lives on through them. Wherever there is a burning-bush voice of God that consumes the heart but not the faith, Moses lives on.

What kinds of heroes die before the final triumphant scene into the Promised Land? God's kind of heroes. Jesus died. All had forsaken him and fled. Jesus died alone, misunderstood, misjudged— a fallen hero. Jesus died the death of a traitor. Jesus—a hero of a new movement with nothing but new hope—died. Some folks have tried to discredit him, century after century; some have made this hero an idol. Some have made museums in his name and called them churches;

some have relettered his words and called them inerrant. But the people who know him best are the ones moving on toward the land of healing and hope that he showed to us. The people who know him best are traveling on the rocky road of peace and justice. The people who know him best are bound for the Promised Land. The people who know him best haven't stopped to build a museum or spruce up the burial site for admission. The ones who know him best are people moving on toward the Promised Land.

You know some people like that? I do. My heroes are here. Right in front of me. Ordinary people who do extraordinary and heroic acts in the name of Jesus Christ. God's people bound for the Promised Land is who you are. Let's keep going.

This sermon was preached in January 1992 at Prescott Memorial Baptist Church of Memphis, Tennessee.